He Walks Like a Cowboy

He Walks Like a Cowboy

One Man's Journey Through Life With a Disability

Jonah Berger

iUniverse, Inc.
New York Lincoln Shanghai

He Walks Like a Cowboy
One Man's Journey Through Life With a Disability

Copyright © 2007 by Jonah Berger

All rights reserved. No part of this book may be used or reproduced by any means, graphic, electronic, or mechanical, including photocopying, recording, taping or by any information storage retrieval system without the written permission of the publisher except in the case of brief quotations embodied in critical articles and reviews.

iUniverse books may be ordered through booksellers or by contacting:

iUniverse
2021 Pine Lake Road, Suite 100
Lincoln, NE 68512
www.iuniverse.com
1-800-Authors (1-800-288-4677)

Because of the dynamic nature of the Internet, any Web addresses or links contained in this book may have changed since publication and may no longer be valid.

The views expressed in this work are solely those of the author and do not necessarily reflect the views of the publisher, and the publisher hereby disclaims any responsibility for them.

ISBN: 978-0-595-47168-3 (pbk)
ISBN: 978-0-595-91448-7 (ebk)

Printed in the United States of America

For Grandpop.

Acknowledgements

In the writing of this book and the preparation of my spirit in the life leading up to its publication, I humbly wish to thank: Brother Josh (My Impetus), Marc (A best friend whose support around my path is immeasurable and invaluable), Mr. Ladbush, My parents, Chachi, L.B.P., Dre., Ryan Moore (my street-level amazing editor; for helping me turn this from a fragment convention into a book!), Stefanie Jones, Derek Jones, Barry Neville, Amos, Ben, Mr. Woo Chipackai, Aunt Mildred, John Cowan, Diane Kimmell, Annie Kennedy, Dr. Min E. Younx, Brother Joel, Johnny K., Bunny, Mary Balow, Ray Boston, Pete Testerman, Andrea Moore Photography, Ross, Rachael, Chandler, Monica, Phoebe, Joey, the Antelope, Pepito, the Maryland Crew, the Colorado Peeps, my mighty family tree, Adam's Camp et al, Elliot Weintraub, Colorado, my Dad, Styx, love, and God.

Introduction

"It is essential that we cope with the realities of the past and the uncertainties of the future, with a pure and chosen hope."—Mattie J.T. Stepanek

My name is Jonah Berger. I am 35 years old. Born and raised in Maryland, I've lived for the past 8 years in the great state of Colorado. I am a regular man. I go to work, I have friends, and I live my life. The difference is that I live this life of mine with a disability. I have what is called Charcot Marie Tooth, or CMT, a form of Muscular Dystrophy.

In the pages that follow, I humbly share my experience of walking through this life with a disability, including all of the highs and lows that come along with that. I aim to share my perspective and that of my loved ones. Every person with a disability has a unique story to tell, and it is my hope that to read this story is to grant yourself some insight about life lived with a challenge. The story is mine; the theme is universal.

It has been one of the great joys of my life to compile these pages. My truest hope is that in reading this story, some greater understanding, sensitivity, and empathy can be achieved. Thank you for reading.

The Inkling

"I'm a man of God,
Though I never learned to pray,
I walked the pathways of the heart,
Found him there along the way ..."

—Neil Diamond

Chapter 1

The Inkling

I remember one day in middle school. I was in the 6th grade. I remember it in the way that you often remember things from that age, clear in the middle and hazy on the edges. This particular memory has me at home plate, holding a bat, and waiting for the pitch from the other team. Gym class was, as you might expect, not my favorite place in the world. Without realizing exactly why, I remember always knowing that I didn't feel at ease in gym class. I was in the hot seat every day during 5th period. The pitch came over the plate, and after 2 missed swings, I connected with one. The ball was hit over the second baseman. I ran as fast as I could towards first base. I ran, as I did during most of my youth, pretty slowly, and aware of the feeling that something was holding me back. I felt as though my spirit ran a lot faster than my legs. With little trouble, I was thrown out at first and earned my team its third out. We were off to play the field.

This is where the memory gets vivid. I remember going to get my glove. I remember that the walk from the bench to my shortstop position was greeted with some comments from my dissatisfied teammates that were less than complimentary. My classmates had often commented about the way I ran. To their credit, they were armed with no knowledge of my disability, and had the maturity level of Jell-O. Yet on that day, the comments sunk in. I remember getting to my position, leaning over to rest my hands on my knees, and feeling for the first time and very sincerely, that something was wrong with me. That I wasn't just slower or less athletic, I was fundamentally different.

The problem with having a realization like that in the 6th grade is that I had no life experience to work with, no stockpile of wisdom to help defend myself. I had no self-help skills with which to gain some perspective on the limitations of my ability and on the affect that others around me would have on my situation. It would have been a perfect moment to receive a visit from my 35 year old self. "Don't worry kid; this is a blessing in disguise. You are gonna climb mountains someday. You are gonna be stronger from your weakness someday. You're gonna teach others through this struggle someday. Worry not, little man, it really is gonna be alright."

Instead, I was left that day, on that field, to do what I have always done, deal with the frustration, set my course, and go grooving and stumbling on my way down the road.

The Path

"Mama said they was my magic shoes.
They could take me anywhere."

—Forrest Gump

Chapter 2
The Path

It was a school night; I was about 5 years old when my mom and dad called me to a sit-down at the kitchen table. My dad, I remember, had a pen and a yellow pad. The two of them commenced to break the news to me for the very first time, I was going to walk an inherently different physical and emotional path through this life.

My specific memories of that night are few but I do remember them informing me that I had CMT. I remember my father drawing a picture of the human body and trying his best to explain the degeneration of myelin sheath and how that would affect the current of electrical brain messages to my ever-waiting muscles, in his best "5-year old-ease". "The messages from the brain to the muscles are slowed down by C.M.T., and over time, the muscles get weaker because they aren't getting the messages fully and fast enough." In retrospect, they did a superb job of explaining it to me. I distinctly remember not freaking out that night. I have ever since used exact quotes from that conversation to explain my disability to newcomers.

Because CMT is a degenerative condition, the effects show themselves more so with time. My condition and physical prowess decline with time, very slowly, and very steadily. In the first ten or so years of my life, I appeared and functioned in as normal a way as can be expected. You wouldn't have known that I had a disease. I ran and played and had the typical crazed energy of a child. The only time when CMT interrupted my reality was about once every two to three months, when I would go to sleep and wake up an hour or so later with leg muscles striving to bring new definition to the word *aching*. I would cry, my mom would bring in a pillow and place it under my knees, and in time I would fall back to sleep, arising the next morning for another day of blissful normalcy. I was completely unaware that those years would be the only in my life where I would experience the feeling of full strength, of full ability.

From age ten to twenty, I ran the gamut of shoe orthotics: A various collection of materials placed into the shoe to assist or to compensate for feet and ankles that are lacking. At first, a thin foam pad that rested under my feet. Then I moved to a more rigid foam that rose to meet the arch in my foot that CMT was ever heightening. Eventually I was wearing a lace up leather supports for both ankles, and then molded plastic ankle high foot supports. During this 10 year period, I was annoyed with the need for assistance, mildly frustrated by the discomfort of these varying devices. Yet, overall, I wasn't drastically affected by the aids. They were hidden by the height of the average high top sneaker, and so at the very least, I wasn't forced to explain my challenge, not to myself or to others. Looking back on that time, I realize that my walking was definitely getting worse. The greatest affect of CMT for me was on my feet and ankles. The muscles that are affected are those that help to lift the foot off the ground every time one takes a step. To best understand this, place your foot flat on the ground. And while keeping your heel on the ground, lift up your toes and the front of your foot. The muscles that you have just used are the muscles that are most affected by CMT.

From ten to twenty years of age, my feet went from normal to struggling to keep themselves up. The devices in my shoes helped stabilize me to a certain degree, but they did not pick my feet up as much as I needed them to. When I look back at video from my late teens, I see that I was overcompensating for this weakness. I was lifting up my leg higher than the average 15-year old, and flopping my foot down with every step. This disease is so slow to progress that I didn't realize then how bad my walking really was. Just as you barely notice that you are growing taller. I tripped a lot. I was clumsy compared to my friends, but it just didn't really soak in. Or, should I say, I didn't *let* it in. It's amazing what the brain can create when not visually reminded of reality.

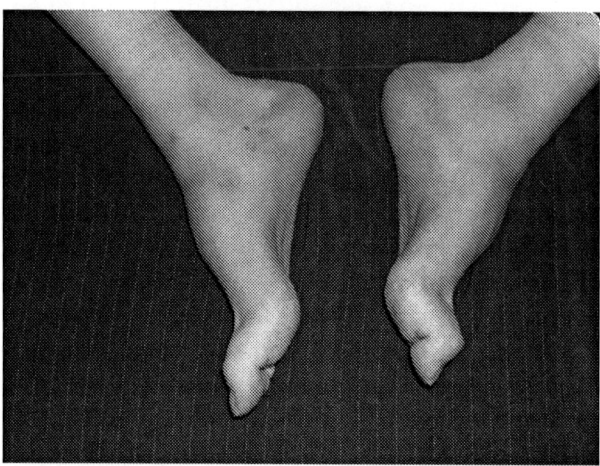

A major chapter in my progression came at the age of 22. The end result of most patients with my level of CMT is the full length AFO (Ankle Foot Orthotic)—a custom-made device made of strong plastic that runs from the top of your calf to the tip of your toe. I was no exception. This mechanism holds my leg, ankle, and foot at a 90 degree angle all of the time, which enables me to walk without the work of lifting my foot. The doctors at the Muscular Dystrophy clinic told me all along that I really should have been in a pair since I was about 15, and I had been telling them what they could do with that notion for about the same amount of time. To me, A.F.O.'s were the enemy. They were the "giving in" of my fight. They were visible from a mile away which would automatically require self-acceptance. And mostly I just felt strong for avoiding them as long as I had. I felt that as long as I stayed away from leg braces, I was still in control, and unwilling to surrender that control to plastic. In my mind, once you accepted the assistance of something so big, I would not be able to go back. I would be dependent on that assistance and therefore, unable to function using my own natural strength.

My 7 year war against this idea came to a halt the day I went for a routine visit to Elliot Weintraub, the man who had designed and created all of the smaller "in the shoe" devices I had used thus far. I was there for my check-up and Elliott, as always, brought up the topic of full length A.F.O.'s. I told him I simply wasn't ready and that we could talk about it in the future. And that is when Elliott made the boldest move anyone ever had in regards to confronting me on my own comfort level. He asked me to try a pair on. He said they had standard test pairs in the office and what did I have to lose by at least trying them on. Elliott had earned enough respect over the years for me to take his challenge. With great discomfort and emotional vulnerability—the likes of my first time naked with the lights on—I put them on and stood up with his help. Elliott instructed me to take a walk down the hall. I took the first step very slowly. I took the second with equal hesitation. And over the next few steps something very magical and quite wonderful took hold. I realized that I was taking steps with a small fraction of the effort that I was so unfortunately used to. The feeling was amazing. It hit me quite literally like a swirl in the stomach. In seconds, I went from a fragile experimenter to a world champion speed walker who had just realized his gift. I liken the experience to the feeling you get when you step onto one of those moving sidewalks that they have in airports. The feeling when you step onto one but keep on walking, and suddenly you can walk faster than normal. Faster than the people who are still on the carpet. That has always given me a rush. And that is how it was for me heading down that office hallway. I was so thrilled; I kept going out the front door of the office and across the parking lot, walking with a speed and fluidity that I hadn't known since I was a child. In that moment, I came to realize one of the greatest lessons that those with a challenge can learn; sometimes, by accepting your weakness and the assistance of an outside source, you can actually accomplish much more than if you rely on pride and deny help. I felt in that moment that with the assistance of these leg braces, I could tap into my real core strength and accomplish physical tasks that were far outside the view of my braceless legs. I turned around, went back into the office, and told Elliott to make me a pair!

This is not to say that welcoming my first pair of leg braces was all magic and stomach swirls; it most assuredly was not. That first pair brought with it a realization of mild, yet consistent discomfort that I would have to tolerate for the rest of my life, both on a physical plane, as well as an emotional one …

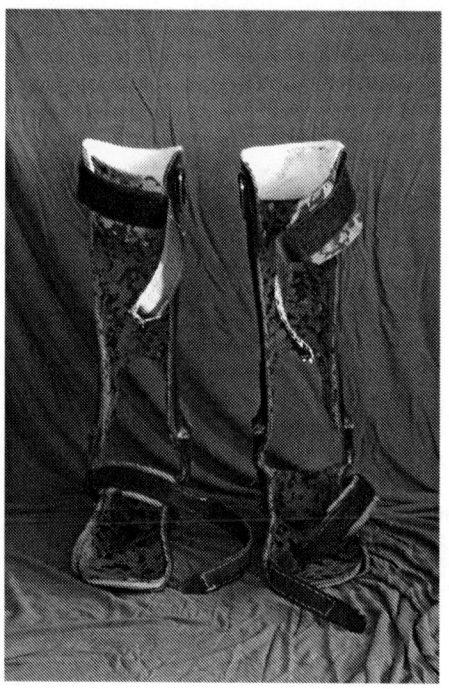

Imagine the sensation of walking around in hard plastic all day. The feeling is all it's cracked up to be. I was introducing myself to a new level of discomfort throughout my day—to a new level of calluses and worn skin. My leg braces over the years have rubbed away enough skin to cover a person completely. The straps that hold the brace to my leg and foot dig in and make themselves heard. The fashion of them is no prize either. I have always loved the look on the brace technicians' faces when I request black straps, or blue foam, as opposed to medical-white, trying to draw out any measure of cool I can from such a distinctly un-cool item. The heat of the brace, especially in the summer, is a force to be reckoned with. I have spent innumerable hours in the offices of various brace companies over the years as they twist, adjust, and tweak my braces to repair the countless cracks and manage the issues that continue to arise. A true soothing of this frustration comes when I find good people to work on my braces. I have been blessed to find just that: A string of devoted individuals that work with me to keep things running smoothly. Over the past few years, due to my increased strength and changing body, I have had more brace trouble than ever before. I am simply putting more wear and weight on them day to day than I was before. Yet I have also come to know the best brace partners anyone could ask for. Dan and Jason (pictured below), have proven to be tireless at finding solutions to my squeaks and clicks. They are the first brace experts who have embraced me for being active and challenged themselves to rise to the occasion. They respect my activity level and are always on board to try and fit the braces to me, and never the opposite. They are the pit crew of dreams!

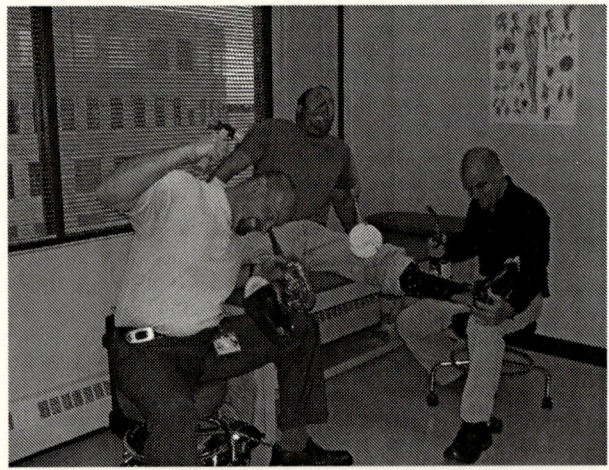

(Dan Irlbeck on the left and Jason Griffin on the right. My torture specialists!)

Another interesting issue in regard to the braces is that as the technology improves, so too do the patients options, which presents major complications. You see, each patient requires different support from their braces. Now, as over 50 styles have arisen, ranging in length, thickness, materials and styles, I am left to try, and thus reject, many pairs before finding the ones that work. I have long dreamed that the engineers of the world would get together and decide on the one brace that is simply "the best". But what I've come to find out is that "the best" is truly subjective. One man's best is another man's nightmare. I've learned that my feet are the true dictators of what they will and will not tolerate. Walk around all day in a pair of A.F.O.'s and your feet will tell you one way or another if they are the right pair. Unfortunately, the only language my feet know to speak in is <u>pain</u>! All of this trial and error has over the years turned me into quite the advocate for myself. I know what feels good and what doesn't. I now have the gumption to look a brace technician in the eye and tell him in no uncertain terms that he needs to do his job differently, sometimes better. Yes, they are the professionals, but I am the *patient*. And not one of the technicians I have met over the years actually has CMT, so without my firm and focused input, they are nothing more than crafty professionals with a lot of plastic and foam. I now view it as my job to help them learn what they need to do with that plastic and foam. It's been an interesting partnership over the years, and it is important for me to note and remember that we have come a long way, to not forget that a few hundred years ago the physically challenged were put away, or left by a stone. Even fifty years ago, they didn't have anywhere near the amazing technology to help get people around. I am lucky to be living in a time when I can push technicians and when those technicians have the tools and education to push back. One could say that in comparison to our history, now is a relatively easy time to be disabled.

Another undeniable fact of the leg brace is that it is easily seen. It is a bold and glaring sign to the world that something is wrong with me and my legs. It is amazing how instantaneously I felt the effects of this. First of all, once I started wearing the braces, my shorts-wearing days came to a screeching halt. Even on the hottest summer day, you would find me in a t-shirt and a full length pair of jeans. At the age of twenty-three, I was happy to choose immeasurable heat over immeasurable embarrassment. When I was in pants, I was OK. I was free to ignore the braces. I was let off the hook from having to answer any questions or yield to any stares. It was a toupee for the legs and I would stay faithful to covering up for the next six to seven years. It wasn't until I was near thirty that I began to see the jeans for what they truly were: a cop out. Since then, and over the past five years, I have pushed myself to try and wear shorts as much as possible in the summertime. This currently translates to about four to five times per year. The number is increasing with time, and the rate of improvement is fine by me. It still boggles my mind though how different I feel when I am wearing shorts. How weak, how exposed. The confidence I have when in long pants is destroyed, and I am wise enough to see that the comfort I have when wearing pants is false. Yet I am so easily drawn to it. I am always amazed at the feeling I get when I have been wearing shorts all day and I first put on long pants. It's as if my disability has been erased and "I'M BACK!" Psychology has a great deal to do with the path of the physically disabled.

The acceptance of A.F.O.'s has lent me quite a few gifts, though. First of all, I have been granted the daily experience of taking them off at the end of a day.

That moment when my leg first pops out of the plastic is almost always greeted with an "Ooooooooh yessssssssss!" and can truly and most closely be compared to a really small orgasm. Secondly, and further addressed in later chapters, as a result of wearing these leg braces, I have accomplished physical feats in my life that I could never have done on my own—the smallest of which is successfully traversing through each day of my busy and mobile life, and the greatest of which is climbing the second tallest peak in the lower forty-eight states, Mt. Elbert, in Leadville, Colorado. Lastly, wearing braces has helped me to see the best kind of beauty. I still appreciate surface beauty, but intrinsically, it is not what matters to me. My braces and general struggle have humbled the high-school superficial nature that seems to be prevalent throughout our society. That is why I have never liked movies whose only selling point is pretty faces. I like movies of pretty character, hot intentions, sexy deeds, and good looking acts of truth. That is what I am most attracted to at the end of the day, because that is what I am requiring others to be most attracted to in me.

The genetics of this disease tend to vary between the different forms of CMT. My family line has CMT 1X. To the best of my ability, I explain it like so: The disease is found on the X chromosome in my family. The men who have it, like me, have it on the X chromosome but also have a healthy Y chromosome. For the females in my family, the disease, if present, is found on one of their two X chromosomes. What does this mean? When a female in my family has a child, there is a fifty percent chance with each child that they will contract CMT. Depending randomly on which of the mother's two X chromosomes are contributed to that child—the healthy X or the affected X. This is shown in the fact that my one sibling, sister Erica, is healthy. Therefore my mother contributed her healthy X to my father's healthy X. And then came me, affected with CMT. My mother contributed her affected X to my father's healthy Y.

My own reproductive opera then sings like so: any female child I have will then also have CMT, since having a female will mean that I have given my affected X chromosome. Any male children I have will not have CMT, as I will have lent my healthy Y chromosome to the process.

The older I get, the more I have come to accept this disability of mine and to attempt, at least, to work in harmony with it. As I grow older, so grows my relationship with this disability. Some insecurities fade away, some cement and grow stronger. Some challenges are overcome, and new ones are born before me. I think a lot about when I become a father. To be a father and not be physically able all of the time is a tough contradiction to overcome. I will need to lean on my wife for the strength a lot of the time. I even worry about tripping when I hold my child someday. These are things that run through my mind. Yet, my emotional and physical progressions are ongoing. And I can do nothing more than try to continually accept my situation. I try to be honest with myself and with others about it. I offer myself the reality that so far and ever more, I will handle it how I handle it. Sometimes with misery, sometimes with great courage, and all of the time, with the highest level of honesty I can attain.

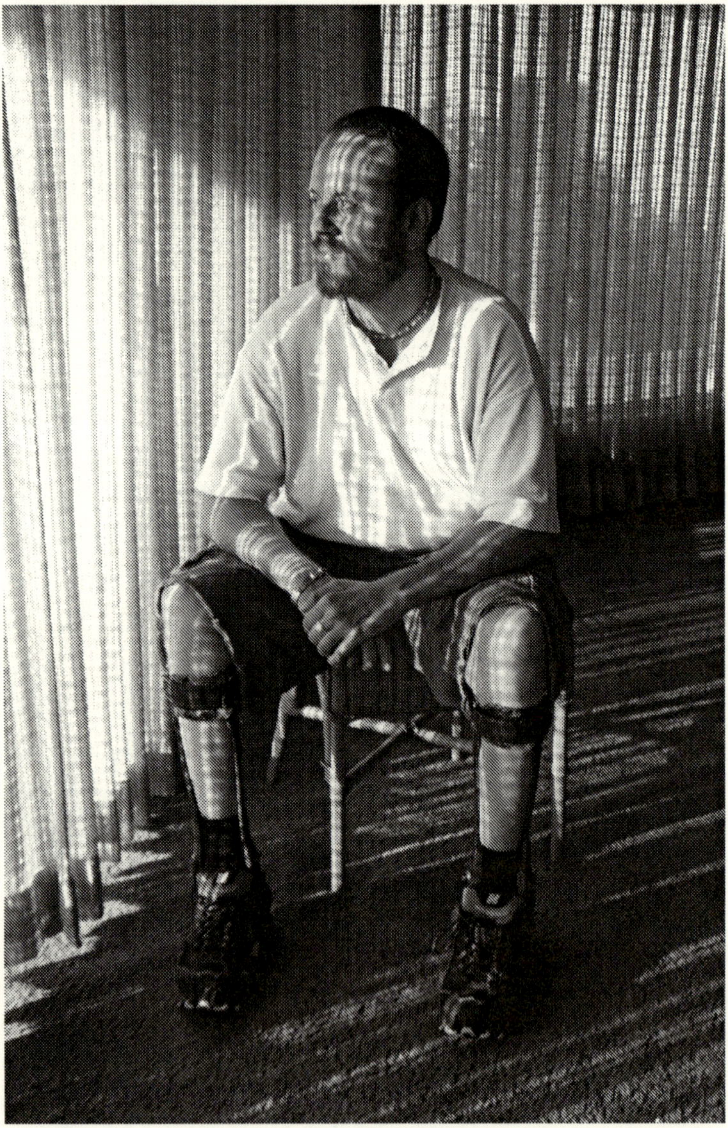

12   He Walks Like a Cowboy

Marching to the Beat of My Own Drummer

"The original Drumbeat is the beat of your own heart."

Mickey Hart
Drummer; The Grateful Dead

Chapter 3

Marching to the Beat of My Own Drummer.

While the largest affect of CMT occurs in the lower legs, ankles, and feet, the other predominantly affected areas are the hands and wrists. As a result of the slowed brain messaging, the muscles in my wrists and hands are weakened over time. The greatest challenge is in regards to what is called "fine motor" or the ability to accomplish smaller physical tasks using the fingers. The reason this is tough for me is twofold. One, as a result of CMT my fingers and toes are slowly curling in, resulting, over many years, in the loss of the loose flexibility of normal digits. In my hands, that is problem number one. The second difficulty has to do with a cluster of muscles located between your thumb and forefinger. This muscle group is responsible for any task that requires your thumb and fingers to work in conjunction. You notice this cluster because on most hands, it is represented by a slightly rounded bulge between the thumb and forefinger on the top of your hand. On my hands, that area is represented by a concave dip revealing just my skin and the shape of my bones. This has left me with a drastic depletion in my ability to do small things like button a shirt, pick up a penny, or effectively squeeze a lime into my drink. It provides for interesting irony. I can lift a barbell of 100 pounds, but I can't pick a safety pin off the ground.

A few major breakthroughs of "leg brace" proportion have come in regard to my hands. The smaller of the two is the button hooker. This is not a cute prostitute. No, this is a device that consists of a large graspable rubber handle and a small metal extended piece. The metal piece is inserted through the hole side of the shirt and then hooks the button allowing me to pull it through the hole. Quite a handy device, actually. I see it that way now. Yet, like most forms of assistance, it was hard to embrace for the proud and needy. From the ages of fifteen to twenty-five, as my hands and fingers slowly started to weaken, I continued to button my shirts the way I always had. The weaker I got, the slower the buttoning became, and the greater number of episodes when I would spend five full minutes working on one small button, screaming obsenities at the top of my lungs. I am sure that my neighbors back then did not think I was much of a morning person.

The grander hand breakthrough came just after college. I was camping with a group of friends and late one evening, under the Western Maryland sky, next to a lively campfire, a good friend of mine named Dan offered me a drum to play alongside some of the other fireside instruments that were in full swing. I accepted and sat with the drum between my legs for a while before I started to play along. Before long, I found myself in one of those life moments that simply unfold before you, as if you are watching it on a screen with no intentional participation whatsoever. In mere moments, I was caught up in the musical groove before me. I was playing along, and what's more, I was playing in rhythm. I was smiling past the confines of my face in that moment delighted to discover two previously unknown pieces of my soul within the same moment. One, I had rhythm. A clear and natural inclination towards percussion. And two, I was using my *hands* to create that rhythm. These weak and suffering hands were in full swing and focused accomplishment. I noticed the joy I was deriving from using my hands in a way that was good and strong and righteous. I felt great.

That was in 1995, and in the twelve years since, I have become a drummer. Playing casually around many campfires for my friends, using percussion in my work with children over the years, and most proudly, drumming in a folk/bluegrass band from 2003-2005. I never really attempted or took to kit drumming, the set-style of drums you sit behind and play with sticks. I think holding and grasping the sticks would be too much strain over time. That is why I have always stayed partial to hand drumming—using just my hands to beat various Latin and African drums. There are many wonderful gifts that come from drumming: a chance to feel connected to rhythm, a chance to express myself musically, a chance to join a band and play on stage in front of people, the ability to entertain others, the opportunity to connect to other drummers and musicians, peace, love, and so on. I do think the most special gift that I have derived from my drumming is the relationship it has caused me to form with my hands. Before drumming, I noticed that I simply didn't want to think about my hands. I didn't want to focus on them. I kept my eyes off of them unless I was forced to. Yet the act of drumming, in a very natural way, brought some much needed focus back to them. While I was drumming, I would feel proud of my hands. When I was done drumming, I would think of my hands as slightly more rugged. And most especially, I have adopted a unique style of hand drumming, mostly different from the true professionals and from the way it is taught in lessons.

You see, true hand drumming requires finesse. After taking several hand drumming lessons, I came to learn that it requires a lot more finesse than one would expect. It requires very delicate ways of forming your hands and shaping them to get just the right tone from the drum and using very precise and varying amounts of force with each hit you make in order to achieve the different tones that any one drum head contains. But finesse is not a word I often associate with C.M.T. Most things that require true finesse are the things that cause me the most difficulty. While I was taking these lessons, I found that I couldn't shape my hands in the traditional ways they were preaching. I couldn't use my fingers to achieve various sounds. I naturally ended up with a "If you can't finesse em', smack the hell out of em'" style. I found myself naturally compensating with force for what I could not achieve with finesse. I played my drums loud, and hard. I went after the rhythm with a vengeance. And while I have never considered myself to be all that great a drummer, I found that those I played for enjoyed my groove as a result of its difference. I think they pick up on my intensity, and it is contagious. I have, over time, explored ways to work within this style to achieve the common tones, in my uncommon ways. I am not able to get it all yet, but I do find that I have learned to hold my own. When I watch a traditional hand drummer play it amazes me. It is very different than the way I play, and it reassures me of the accomplishment that my hands have figured out their own way to play. Nice going, boys!

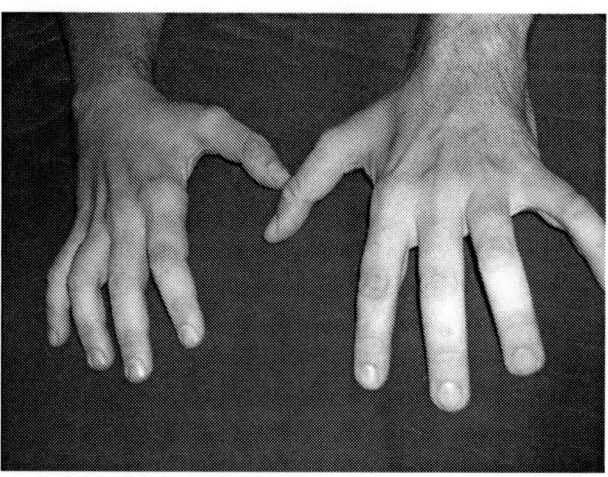

This part of my path has taught me one of the most important and common lessons to those with physical challenges: in most cases, you will be able to accomplish whatever you wish; the trick is understanding that you may have to accomplish them in very *different* ways than other people. Accepting that it is the destination that matters, not how you arrive there. I use a button hooker as most people use their fingers. I use my two pointer fingers to pick up small items as most people use their finger and thumb. It is amazing to me just how much precious energy I have spent over the years struggling with tasks that could quite easily be accomplished by the swallowing of pride, by the accepting of difference. The more I focus my attention on the best way to get things done, as opposed to the most *normal* way, the easier life becomes. Simple as that. And the beat goes on …

The Ladies

"I'm beginning to see that the adjective we should be striving for is less so, 'Confident',
And more so, 'Aware'."

−Journal entry, 2007

Chapter 4
The Ladies

When it comes to being with women in combination with a physical disability, it became clear to me early on that I wasn't going to be able to rely on physical prowess to get the attention of the opposite sex. In regards to *the song of me*, girls were going to have to listen to the words; the tune alone wasn't gonna do it. In the discussion of this topic, it is helpful and important to cite specific women who have played a part in my development of balance between women and disability. To preserve their anonymity, I have chosen to call them each by a certain dessert. Why? Because each one of these precious souls have been a very sweet turn on this life path of mine.

I have always seen a certain benefit to my disability and how it pertained to my pursuit of the opposite sex. CMT being a degenerative condition, allowed a certain sense of "normalcy" in the early years of my pursuit. I had basic and common physicality and ability during the all too crucial teenage years. The fact that CMT wouldn't truly show itself until years later allowed me to deal only with the typical awkwardness of youth instead of compounding that strange time with the affect of a physical challenge. I was no all-star athlete, but I have a feeling that CMT had little to do with that. So I began, thank God, to use my humor and personality to attract the girls in my line of sight. And to thank God again, I was blessed with enough charisma to obtain a series of normal, youthful experiences on my growing path. Then came the middle stages, when I was still appearing mostly "normal". Around the ages of fifteen to twenty-one, the physical manifestations of CMT were starting to surface. In my mid teens, it would be falling down sometimes, tripping over my own feet on ground that could not have been flatter. Take one of my first girlfriends ever; we'll call her "Pudding." Pudding was a great early example of sheer immaturity. I remember falling down in front of her once and she was too busy laughing at first to think of any potential concern for me. To her credit, she was fifteen. And also to her credit, she was not armed with any information from me in regards to my condition. I was years away from wanting to talk to a woman about it. Pudding was also a lot richer in looks than she was in heart. Sorry, Bill Cosby.

Then there was the first time I fell in love, at the age of 17. This wonderful soul, we'll call "Sherbet." Sherbet was great. She was beautiful on the inside and out. She was my first experience with the flood and range of emotions that accompany a solid tumble. We were together on and off for 2 years. Sherbet helped me to understand one very important reaction in the many I would receive over the years when confronting a woman with the reality of my disability. The dreaded, "Uncomfortable Silence" response. I was just entering into my true openness about my condition, and because we were so close for so long she was well aware of my condition. Yet, as time passed by, I began to notice that she never brought it up. It was never addressed by her directly or in any other way, for that matter. Over time this was beginning to get to me. It came to a head one evening when we were together, and intimate, and I chose that honest space to ask her forthright, "How do you feel about my disability?" Sherbet went flat faced. Her expression was one of discomfort and desire to hop the next helicopter ride instantly out of that corner. She replied with some very brief and unemotional one-word answers, along the lines of "fine", and "o.k.". I remember that moment very well. I remember it because I was absorbing several realities all at once. 1. I was pissed at her and annoyed with her lack of reassurance. 2. I felt for her, for not having the natural reactive sensitivity to my situation. 3. I respected that youth had a role to play in her not being ready to handle such reality in the midst of our naked youthful freedom. 4. The most important reality of all in that moment: I instantly absorbed the fact that because of my condition, I was not going to be able to connect with just any woman. It was going to take a woman of strong sensitivity. Of solid empathy. Of true vision, to see past the disability and right through to where the truth of the matter resides. My heart.

I remember feeling sad about that in the moment. As if, to some degree, the party was over. The age of ignorance and denial were coming to an end. In retrospect, it was a true blessing. That night with Sherbet was the beginning of truth—the start of a new path in regards to women, a path where there was no keeping CMT from them, no hiding it, and therefore, no constant worry about its escape. I was now starting to sense a new plan—an easier ride. A simpler way of being more up front with women about CMT and therefore knowing up front when a "potential partner" was not up for dealing with my condition. It was essential to become aware of those women early on, and not wait over a year to find out. Because believe you me, it will come out eventually. I also realized that to be truthful in the beginning helped to signal me when I had found a keeper. If the initial reaction was good, and sensitive, I knew at least that I had found a sweet girl. A girl of substance. A girl worthy of the attempts to bridge all of the other gaps between two people. In many ways, this disability of mine is a truth filter. It is an undeniable bridge to cross if you want to share my heart. Those who are able to cross the bridge are allowed in. And those who are not able are naturally filtered from my life. It is a good tool when looked at in that regard.

Since that night, and since turning twenty-one, the theory has proven true. I have, with age, intensified in my physical sensitivity, and my sleeve-worn truth about it. With the welcoming of leg braces, and the weakening of my muscles, I was forced to deal with my condition on a more constant, realistic, and open basis—both with myself, and in turn, with others. It was tricky, though, because when I was wearing long pants, and in good physical form, it was still relatively easy to pass as "normal", which was a constant temptation to conceal my disability from women to whom I was attracted. It is amazing how much I was growing bolder in certain areas, yet wearing long pants and shying away from my truth in others. The term "weakness" has always been synonymous with "not getting the girl" in my mind (not to mention throughout our culture.) The strength and physique that are portrayed as girl-worthy were growing farther and farther away from the man I was becoming. I felt that the appearance of my braces would shine with weakness, dependency, and a general sense of "less".

The same is true with my hands. As they have grown weaker, so has my self-consciousness with them in regards to women. There were several women I dated during these mid twenties years, and each one of them not only crossed the bridge to me, but also allowed me to work on my own comfort and ease with this condition. They helped me through struggle and joy, to slowly learn that I couldn't rely on looking strong; I simply had to be strong. Those few women that I dated during that time helped me a great deal. Much love goes out to "Cupcake," "Bananas Foster," and "Jell-O."

The greatest amount of growth I have made in the sharing of my disability with women was achieved with two wonderful women with whom I have had the honor to connect. We'll call them Flan and Flambé. Both of these women taught me amazing things about myself and my relationship to my disability. Their lessons were very different based upon the differences in who *they* were. I fell in love with Flan when I was twenty-seven. She and I had been friends for some time and it grew from there. Flan was a really great breakthrough for me because she was my first taste of a woman who could care for my disability completely as if it made no difference to her whatsoever. The bonus of Flan was that though she had not dated a man with a disability before, she took to it like it was adjusting to my height or the color of my eyes. She would ask me questions about my experience. She would seek out reading materials about my disability to become more informed. She sought out special socks for me to keep my feet well cushioned. She used me as an opportunity to grow and to become more aware. Flan taught me that it was time to raise the bar when it came to whom I would make a connection. It was no longer just going to be about accepting my disability. It was going to be about embracing it. The bar deserved to be raised that high, and it hasn't been lowered since.

The next great push forward in my love path was with Flambé, named for the warmest relationship I have had since embracing my disability. In addition to being a wonderful person, Flambé, by my stroke of good luck, came from a history of dealing with difference. Flambé has a brother and a nephew with Down's syndrome. She is also a speech-language pathologist, so she had dedicated her career to assisting those who are in need of help. Flambé has literally grown up sensitive to these differences and the struggles they create. It is her only reality. Once I realized that I loved this person, I soon after realized how easy it was going to be with her. Flambé was going to be my oasis, my well-deserved first experience with complete and total ease. I was afforded the experience of total comfort with my disability in the presence of a woman I was crazy about. She made it easy for me to share it with her. I fluidly ignored my usual defenses around the topic. It was a rush. She held my feet at the end of the day and rubbed them, with love in her eyes. This is the absolute dream for a man with a disability—to have a woman so true of heart to walk alongside him.

About a year into our relationship, Flambé and I went camping with a group of our friends. We were out hiking, when we came upon a creek. It wasn't that wide across, but it was steep. It was clear that we would have to leap over it to avoid wet feet. One by one, my "normal" friends leapt over the creek, and then it came down to me. I made my best effort but landed my rear foot completely into the cold mountain water. The reaction of the others proved of great interest to me. All but Flambé snapped into motion to offer assistance and to check if I was alright. Flambé stood her ground and was laughing at the event. To her it was funny. As soon as the others heard her laugh, they turned their reactions to her. Flambé, in the purity of her intent, explained that she trusted me to ask for help if I needed it, and besides, it was funny. In a beautiful way, in the best of all ways, she was right. She knew me; if I needed help I would've asked for it. If I was truly hurt, she would have known. That not being the case, she laughed, the way we do when watching people fall into water on "America's Funniest Home Videos". The bottom line is that it was funny. And in Flambe's strange style, she was showing me the truest form of respect by not treating me like a helpless case that needed to be tended to because his foot was wet. She treated me like a man. She honored my normalcy and my ability, as opposed to highlighting or dramatizing my inability. It is a gesture I dare say I'll not forget. Although I am no longer with Flambé, I will always hold her dear to my heart for many reasons, one of which was allowing me to feel completely at ease with my disability.

The lesson that has come in the most recent years of my life is this: Flan and Flambé were trying to show me that a real woman is most interested in who you are, in the strength of your character, in the sincerity of your heart. A real woman is not concerned with the strength of your muscles. While physical prowess is a nice bonus, it is not the stuff that true love is made of. It is not the foundation on which reality stands. And in essence, I am strong at the end of the day. It takes a great deal of ability to be disabled in this world. It requires a physical and emotional toughness that many "men" will never know. It is my job and should be my goal to be honest with women, to be forthright about my situation, and most of all, to feel good about my disability. Not about its effects, it's hard to feel good about tripping and sore feet. It's not hard to feel good about who I am and to never cower from my reality. I am a man with a disability. I need assistance sometimes. I need to vent my frustration sometimes. I need to share my life and heart with a woman who will support me, who will challenge me. One who will not think less of me. And if it turns out to be a bit harder to find that woman because of my condition, well then so be it. There is simply no other way for me. Like all things, I simply have to live the "normal" experiences in my abnormal way. My "manly strength" will come from walking around in hard plastic every day for the rest of my life. I will be strong by accepting the many ways that I need assistance. I will be a true man by living my life in truth. Not in fear or shame. In bold, challenge-attacking, never-quitting, weakness accepting, pure-hearted truth. Onward.

Mt. Elbert and the Children of Truth

"It's interesting, due to my physical challenge, my thumbs aren't very useful. I used to see both of my thumbs as weak. But recently, my right thumb is much worse. The right side in general is worse off. So now my left thumb, having the same strength it did before, has become the "strong" thumb, compensating for the struggling right one. A lot of what strength is, is just perception."

—Journal entry from 1996

Chapter 5

Mt. Elbert and the children of truth.

It is 5:15am on August 10, 2003. I am standing in the dark at the trailhead of Mt. Elbert in Leadville, Colorado. At the time, I was a youth treatment counselor for a Denver-based agency called Tennyson Center for Abused and Neglected Children. Some of the kids at the agency were part of a summer adventure group called "Challenge by Choice". The staff, myself included, could sign up to be additional support on one of the ten trips the C.B.C. kids take over the summer. In the spring of 2003, I reviewed the list of potential trips I could help with and noticed this Mt. Elbert hike. It was slated to be later in the summer, and Elbert seemed a friendly enough name, so I signed up. I calmly penned my signature to accompany twelve kids up the second tallest peak in the lower forty-eight states. I unknowingly signed up for what would become the hardest and greatest day of my physical journey!

I fumble with my tiny headlamp trying to get my 5a.m. brain to accomplish even this menial task. Eventually, my light comes on, and I take the first steps up the dark and wooded path. The recommended time for this eight mile, 4,500 foot vertical climb is eight hours. I would return back down to that very point at 7:30p.m. Fourteen hours later. Fourteen very long and amazing hours later.

The beginning few hours of the walk were like a steady and gradual hike through the woods. Many trees, a clear path, and the benefits of fresh legs. I had a decent night's sleep, several weeks of training through walks around my neighborhood, and all the wide-eyed optimism of a proud thirty-one year-old. As the sun rises, the temperature warms, and the headlamps are put to rest. I am one of seven staff members accompanying twelve kids up the mountain. Each staff was assigned to one or two of the kids, and I drew the luck of Jasmine. Jasmine was a tough teenager. She was sweet, creative, and quite scarred from the troubles of her youth. She was a strong kid physically and was clearly able to handle this trek. She was partnered with the one staff member who had a disability. It turned out to be a destined partnership.

As we trek through the woods, heading for the tree line, it becomes quickly clear who is going to sail through this day and who is going to bitch through it. A few of the staff/child combos are already well ahead of the others. A few combos are well behind. There are some kids who sense what they've gotten themselves into, and they react with defeat. I am already sensing similar vibes, but I keep my reactions to myself. I decided that I was going to summit this mountain. I had also, in advance, decided that I wasn't going to quit in front of these kids. I was going to have a brave face. I was going to prove to them what a man can do, even with a disability. *Especially* with a disability. So I walked on. With Jasmine an understandable 10-20 feet in front of me, we move on. I remember taking our first break amidst those woods, and I remember feeling what the breaks would do to my emotions. As soon as I sat down, I felt that desire to stay there forever. I started negotiating how long I would allow myself to stay there. Half of me relaxing and drinking water, and the other half, bartering with the daunting task still ahead. In retrospect, the amount of breaks we took was appropriate, and they allowed us all to talk to each other about life, about ourselves, and about what we were going through. It was on the second of these breaks, just before the tree line, that we had our first snack—a peanut butter and jelly sandwich. That sandwich tasted so damn good that I remember it to this day. Eating out of pure visceral necessity comes with a greater level of pleasure than eating because it is lunch time. My whole body tasted the food. My whole body enjoyed the food. It was literally fuel for the machine. While sitting on a rock with Jasmine and a few others, she looked at me, first in the eyes and then down at my feet and asked, "You alright?" I understood her in that moment. She was letting me know that she knew I was in the midst of a great challenge. She knew I was nervous. She saw through the façade and decided to let me know that she was not some naïve kid. I told her I was fine. I told her that the day was going to be tough for me, but that I was gonna walk up that mountain come hell or high water. She was a smart kid.

We walked on; it was starting to get a little warm. Then, after almost 3 hours, we reached the tree line. The point of altitude when the air becomes so thin that plants, including trees, cannot grow. It's an impressive sight. In about 20 feet of space, you go from woods to open mountain side. This was the point when our first few kid/staff teams dropped out. It had just become too much for them. And for some kids, just getting on that mountain and trekking up it for 3 hours was the true peak. It provided additional motivation for me to get up that hill, though. Now I was walking for those who couldn't. I was also walking a little tougher to fight against the ever-looming quitting vibe that was starting to capture a few of the group. The distance to the tree line is stage one—gradual wooded hiking. The next stretch is stage two—a steeper section of the mountain where to best traverse it, the path is designed in a switchback formation. A giant and wide swiping "S" path leading straight ahead. It implies that it spreads your oxygen and energy more efficiently to walk back and forth and increase your elevation slowly, as opposed to walking straight up. This became a test of my endurance. I was starting to get tired. I was also weighed down by the fact that I had NO idea how far I had to go. In prime Jonah-fashion, I pulled out my sense of humor to battle against the building sense of monotony and exhaustion. I made jokes to make myself laugh. I made jokes to make the kids laugh. It was my way of staying sane and letting the kids know that I was alright and still strong, and maybe letting myself know the same thing. This was actually an enjoyable stretch of the trip for me. We all talked a lot. We laughed a lot. It was good to hang out with these kids and staff away from the normalcy of our building. There is something that begins to happen amongst people who are challenged together, especially amidst nature. There is a slow bond that forms. It is a good bond. And Stage two really kicked it in for me. It was a bond I would come to rely upon more and more as we continued up the mountain.

When we were about halfway up the mountain, my dogs started to bark a bit. I was definitely feeling the lower levels of oxygen and starting to require more frequent breaks. My spirits were high, though, and I got the sense that I was participating in a grand experience, the likes of which I had never tasted. It was starting to get interesting to me, and a little exciting. Then I looked up and met stage three—the shortest and steepest stage of them all. It consists of a tall and steep pile of rocks. It is so tall that you can't see past it. No sight of what lays beyond. And it was instant panic to me when I realized that I was about to change my title from mountain hiker to rock climber. I don't mean to imply that it was the top of Everest and equipment was required to scale it, but for a total novice like me, these were big rocks and the path to get over them was not clear. I was truly nervous for the first time that day. The jokes stopped, the focused planning began, and the "Rocky" theme began to play in my head. Over the next hour I proceeded to climb, over one big rock at a time. This is when my disability began to really show itself.

Balance is the grand issue for me. I am not comfortable jumping from one rock to another, thus my standard style usually works out to be more of an "all 4's" situation. I am like a cat that uses both arms and legs to brace myself. I was scaling each rock instead of standing on them. Some were easy, some were a bit tough. A few were downright scary. My heart pounded and my fear was alive. But, to the tune of the day, I kept going. I remember stage three being one of solitude. I sort of tuned out the others and went into my own mode of focus, my own zone. Jasmine, who was complaining a bit, required little hand holding. She was heading up those rocks at a solid pace. The other staff on the trip were of immeasurable assistance to me. Several of them were pivotal in getting me up that mountain. The greatest of which was Audra, a dear friend and head of the CBC group. She knew of my disability well. She watched my process as I headed up the hill. She would check in on me from time to time and make sure I was still smiling. She was working to get up that hill as well, but when she realized that the rocks of stage three were throwing me around a bit, she came and took my pack from me until I reached the top of the rocks. This was Audra, the finest kind.

Another staff member of solid note was Caley. Just as we reached the top of the stage three rock pile, one of the kids decided that they had had enough. He was crying and clearly beyond our attempts to verbally motivate him to move on. At this point in the trek, all of the remaining hikers had formed into one group. A few had darted right up to the top; a few had fallen back and stopped below, but the rest of us middle grounders were traveling as a crew now. So when it became clear that one of the kids needed to head back down, it became clear as well that a staff member would have to join him. There were four staff with this group and we all had come so far and wanted to summit. It was one of those moments when everyone should volunteer and no one wants to. I remember Caley looking at me and speaking up that she would take the kid back down. I got a very sincere sense that she appreciated the importance of me getting up that mountain, and she sacrificed her own summit in exchange for my own. I have never forgotten that.

The time had come to roll on. We entered stage four—the final and by far the toughest stage of them all, physically, mentally, and emotionally. Physically because the air is thin. Very thin. And the work of hiking uphill causes you to breathe at an elevated level because you are simply not getting the amount of oxygen that you require. Therefore, you breathe quicker. The frequency of rest stops begins to increase again. We took shorter but more frequent breaks, stopping to just be still for a few minutes and then moving on. The higher up we went, the worse it got. We were approaching 14,000 feet at this point. It got so that at times, I would take three to four steps and have to stop for a breather (pardon the pun). The exhaustion of the combined efforts from stages one through three in addition to the ever-thinning air made for a truly daunting physical challenge. Mentally, the higher I went up the mountain, the more evenly distributed the challenge became between physical and mental. The physical is an underlying current throughout the journey, but the mental really comes into play near the top. It takes a great deal of focus and belief to keep walking when you can't breathe and your feet feel like throbbing personalities all their own. I had been walking uphill for hours. All I wanted to do was sit down, that was when the mental fight came into play. I have always loved the mental fight, because it is the one fight that my disability cannot touch. It is the side of my strength where I can dictate the intensity. It is my opportunity to kick ass. And while it is very difficult at times, it is something I have come to rely upon. My weak muscles take me only so far, the strength of my will takes me the rest of the way.

Lastly, is the emotional struggle. This came into play in what they call *false peaks*. In retrospect, I call them "insanity-makers." There are three of them in stage four. False peaks mean that in the distance, you see what appears to be the top of the mountain. It is far away, but at least you have it in sight. You walk 3-5 steps at a time. You gasp to breathe with any semblance of normalcy, but you walk on. The closer to this peak you get, the happier you become. The jubilation builds, the end, or so you think, is truly in sight. Until you reach these rat bastard peaks, and take that final step on to it, only to look up and far away and see the true peak of the mountain, (or so you think). All three of these false peaks were killers to the emotional side of this voyage. I heaped so much of my hope and energy onto reaching the top, and I was so tired, that the moment when I realized there was still a long way to go, it broke me a bit. Like paroling an inmate, and as he walks through the gate, there is a sign that says, "Just kidding, ten more years pal."

I found myself doing a lot of cursing inside my head. I may have been on my last nerves, but I was still a staff member. I kept the cussing to myself. After the last false peak, I looked up and saw the top. I checked with a few downward climbers to confirm its true identity. They assured me it was the real deal. I walked on. I remember that last stretch being a bit hazy. I was starting to feel the effects of sustained oxygen deprivation. I took one step at a time. I took about five to seven breaths between each step. Every ten minutes or so, Jasmine would walk back to me and say, "Come on Jonah, you can do it!" And after what seemed to be about ten years, I looked up and Audra was standing in front of me smiling, saying "You made it." I was on top of the mountain. I was standing 14,433 feet above sea level. I gave Audra a hug. Within seconds I started to cry, I turned away from the kids and walked off on my own. I had just accomplished an amazing feat for someone with my condition. And what's more, I had drastically stretched my own boundaries. I became tougher that day. I realized in that very moment that CMT did not have to define my ability. It factors into my ability, certainly, but I learned in that moment that I had the final say in this life of mine—not the disability. When it came right down to it, my mind and heart were mightier than my challenge. It was a beautiful lesson to learn, one that has stayed with me ever since. It was one that I couldn't learn unless I was willing to push myself well past the confines of my comfort. With risk came grand reward. No tears can ever be more aptly described as tears of joy than the ones streaming down my face in that moment. Beautiful tears filled with awareness. Giants tears made of strength discovered. Free tears of a man standing on top of the world. I decided to go back and join the group, still crying. It was a good decision. The kids all congratulated me. They all were well aware of the moment. They clearly had pride for me and I was glad to have shared the moment with them.

The view from the top was so profound that mere words would do it no justice. I remember standing up there trying to focus, trying to sharpen the scope of my vision. I tried to frame the picture, and it couldn't be done. It was too beautiful, too vast, and too majestic for simple eyes to conquer. I decided to let my eyes relax and enjoy the hazy blurry serenity of the view. I walked over to the place where they keep a ledger for all who summit to sign. I wrote something about my disability and my grandfather. I was so happy up there. I was standing amidst the strong. I was enjoying the accomplishment. We took pictures and hugged a lot. We ate some and sat a great deal, and after about thirty minutes, it became clear to me that I was only halfway done with my trip. The party was over. We had to get moving to make it down before dark. I was, to say the least, not looking forward to the journey down. My feet hurt. My legs were jelly and I was simply out of chutzpah.

I can summarize the walk down for you like so:

1. Any fool who thinks that the walk down will be easy is as wrong as Dirty Dancing 2—Havana Nights. The pressure of each pounding step on your already tired knees is worse on the way down. It gets worse the farther down you go.

2. Because of my balance troubles, anytime the path got steep, I would simply sit down and crabwalk over the terrain. At times, I was literally sliding down on my butt. I have a hole in the pants I wore that day to prove it. I would rather be down than fall down. Less distance to fall is a good thing for me. It's a thought I always have when hiking: I don't mind falling on the way up because if I fall, I just hit the mountain in front of me. But if I fall on the way down, I have gravity and momentum working against me.

3. As the walk got longer, my patience grew drastically shorter. I all but forgot about Jasmine and the others. I went into my own world of bitter resentment. I was done. My body and spirit were gone and I had at least several hours more to walk. The cussing came out of my head and through my mouth with the reckless abandon of a drunken sailor. I didn't care anymore, and the only moments that I felt half decent were when I would stop and say, "F**K!" The word fit the moment to a T.

4. My good friend Rachael, one of the staff members, literally talked me down the hill. She was a ways in front of me and would call back reports of what was coming next. They were encouraging reports. Slightly false reports, but kind ones. She would stop and wait for me once in a while.

She'd ask how I was doing, she's listen to me bitch, and then we would move on. Cheers, friend.

I turned a corner amidst the trees and I remember crossing a bridge—the very bridge I was standing on while fumbling with my head lamp at 5a.m. I looked in front of me and there was a car waiting for me, with the back door open. It was a sweet sight. I think I may have been aroused by it.

I acquired several pieces of wisdom through the events of that day: the bravery of the self, the necessity of others, and the importance of challenge. Perhaps the most special of all, was the sincerity of children. In looking back on that day, it wasn't my brave face I remember. It wasn't my ability to hide my weakness from the kids. It was the ease with which those kids took to my situation, with no judgment, no bias. They simply knew, and they received me well. It is thanks to the beauty of those kids that I was able to be so free that day, able to save my strength for the mountain and not waste it on a happy façade. This gets me to thinking that kids have always been that way in regards to my disability. Kids have always handled my disability better than adults ever have. Being a childcare worker my whole life has kept me surrounded by children. At every stage of my disability and in my growth with it, I have had to be open about it to the children in my care. They have made that process very easy on me. Kids are very matter-of-fact. They are happy to hear what the deal is. They ask questions and do their investigating, and then they are cool. They move on, armed with true knowledge, and they treat you normally. Ever since I have worn the leg braces, I have always been amazed by kids, especially the little ones. They see my braces and come up and touch them, feel them, ask about them. "Why you got these things on your legs?" And then I tell them, "I was born with legs and feet that aren't very strong, so I wear these to help protect them." Then I always bang on them to show the toughness of the plastic and I ask, "Do you think anything is gonna hurt my legs through these?" They always say, "NO!" My point is made, and we move on. Once they understand, it is no longer an issue, and it rarely ever comes up again. Kids are so unencumbered by politeness. They just say what's what. Typically, I think this is one of their best qualities. Usually adults, in the effort to make sure I don't feel uncomfortable, make me feel twice as uncomfortable. They look at my braces and then quickly look away as if to imply they weren't staring. But they were—and they should. It's different and interesting. It's our human nature to investigate what we see. Especially if it is not a normal sight. My preference then is for strangers to come right to me and ask, like the kids do. Empathy and information eases judgment and helps people of different lives coexist. The truth and boldness I have seen from kids over the years has helped me to better embrace an ease with CMT. It certainly also played a vital role in getting me up that mountain. Thanks, Jasmine: I love you.

(Me, at the summit of Mt. Elbert)

The Learning to Be Open

Whose dwelling is the light of setting suns, whose message is the breeze of sky,
Whose truth is prematurely known, whose song a lullaby,
Whose abled hands a crippled knot, whose readied heart alone,
Whose company is silent fear, whose when's are still unknown,
Whose knights are trees so tall and wise, whose table made of fire,
Whose chivalry is much alive, whose passion shall inspire,
Run to me through grassy fields, Free your arms and leave the ground,
Tis by listening dear friends and listening true,
That the answers we seek can thus be found....

—Jonah Berger

Chapter 6
The Learning to be Open

In a lifetime of amazing influences and terrific people crossing my path, it is interesting how a handful stand out. Some are due to a long-term and profound connection. Others are the result of a pure and true moment that stay with you for the rest of your path. A moment that burns into your soul, and serves as one of the roots of an ever-growing tree.

I met Jason Conn in the summer of 1987. While we would go on to enjoy many years of friendship and a connection that still exists today, the impact that Jason had on my life most powerfully began that first summer, at the age of fifteen. We ended up in summer camp together at Camp Ramblewood in Darlington, Maryland. This is the age when boys are at the peak of their ridiculousness. Young, immature, and self-involved combined with just enough years and ability to get into all sorts of trouble. The highpoint of the fifteen year old's annual spirit explosion is the summertime. I spent all of my summers in camp. It was my favorite place. I was free in camp. I was devoid of any and all responsibility. And I mark that summer as the year I went from a kid to a teen. My eye for the fairer sex was really starting to come into focus. I entered camp that year ready to experiment. Ready to laugh, and ready to celebrate the end of another year of schooling. Enter Jason Conn, the perfect co-pilot for this camp season. A cool cat in every sense of the word. He was smooth and funny, and we made instant partners in crime. He was a good friend to have at fifteen.

I also entered that summer at an interesting point in the development of my disability. I was starting to weaken in my legs and feet. I was starting to walk a little differently than a normal teenage boy. Yet it was nothing drastic and very easily ignored by others and by myself. I hadn't expected to challenge my personal comfort level with CMT at that point. It was always a struggle I assumed I would face in years to come, but had yet to feel ready to really face it. I had certainly not yet experienced the ability to let others into my private well of emotion surrounding my disability. I relied on a steady diet of ignorance and denial.

As the summer wore on, I realized that I was not as able as I had been the summer before. I was stumbling more often. I was losing my balance for lesser reasons than I had before. I felt the struggle starting to set in. I took solace in the accepted teen role of the awkward and un-athletic. Until one afternoon, late in the summer, Jason and I were walking across this field at our camp, and we decided to sit down and relax a bit. I remember sitting in the afternoon sun laughing about one thing or another when out of the blue, Jason asked me, "Why do you walk the way you do?" The question caught me off guard. It's not that I had never bore witness to the stare of others or the laughing when I would trip and fall. It's just that in that very moment, I understood that Jason knew something bigger was going on. In the most incredible way, he was cutting right to the chase. He wanted to know what was up with me.

To my surprise in that moment, and in retrospect ever since, I started right into it. I decided not to think and simply to answer. I decided to be honest for the absolute first time with any friend I had ever had. I told Jason that I had a disability. I told him that I had a form of Muscular Dystrophy. I told him that it was hereditary and that it was passed down to me through my mom's side of the family. The more I talked the easier it came. But I never looked at Jason. I simply looked straight ahead. I told him that it was progressive. I told him that the stumbling and tripping he had noticed was the intensifying of this disease. I told him that I was quiet about it because I didn't think anyone our age would understand. And I remember telling him that I hated having it, that it sucked for me to trip and to have to fight for normal balance. I realized after about two or three minutes that Jason hadn't said anything, so I turned around to look at him. He was crying. This fifteen year-old kid was crying for me. He had listened to what I had said and was so taken by it that he was moved to tears. I couldn't believe it. It was the boldest act of teen honesty and vulnerability that I would ever witness. He told me that he was sorry I had to deal with it. He let me in on how much he could tell something was going on. He told me that he was really glad I had told him. The feeling of opening up about it and the reception I got in return can only best be described as cool water. I was light as a feather. My disability was light as a feather. I was released from a self-imposed chain. I remember the feeling of happiness in that instant. I literally remember how it felt.

(Jason and I, volunteering at The Muscular Dystrophy Telethon)

It was in that moment that I learned the most valuable lesson I could have learned about dealing with my disability. The lesson was that to try and hide something that can't be hidden is a false pursuit. Those with a keen eye and true heart are going to know that something is wrong with me. And to allow for that, to let others into it, to squelch their assumptions and assessments with true and direct knowledge, was going to be the quickest path to comfort, for myself *and* those around me. It was going to allow me to focus my energy on dealing with my disability, not hiding from it. Jason and his reaction to my confession solidified my understanding of this concept.

In looking back on that moment I often think two things: one, what if I had chosen a lesser friend to open up to for the first time? What if I was received with laughter or discomfort or a change of subject? It could have easily sent me in the other direction, one of closeted emotion and reserved acceptance. And two, I thank God that it was Jason Conn sitting there. I thank God that Jason was such an amazing kid, with a righteous wisdom and maturity well beyond his years. Don't get me wrong: Jason was every bit as harsh and immature and self-involved as the rest of our friends that summer, yet he had a side to him that I was lucky to know. And he showed that side of him at a moment that left me forever changed for the better. Since that very day, I have always strived to be the person I was on that field. To be open. To be forthright and honest. To let people in and therefore let myself out, out of the pressure of concealing the inconcealable. Beyond the great weight of carrying the burden of CMT by myself. And out of the shame that attaches to anything you decide needs to be kept a secret. Jason freed me that day. Jason helped me to free myself. The amount of physical and emotional support I have received from friends over the years as a result of letting them in is simply immeasurable. Never underestimate the power of a single moment.

X-Ray Vision

"Some of my smaller toes curl under as a result of my disability. When I walk barefoot in my apartment over the tiles of my kitchen and bathroom, sometimes my toe will get pinned in the cracks between the tiles. It hurts. I have noticed that sometimes in my reaction to it, I say, "You motherfucker!" or "You son of a bitch!" The cussing is one thing. But the "you" part interests me even more. As if I am mad at someone or something. For the pain, for my disability. For the small odds of stepping right in the crack as opposed to the large and smooth surface area of the tiles themselves. Who am I talking to? To God? To fate? To my toes?"

Journal Entry, October 2006

Chapter 7
X-Ray Vision

There is a certain mentality I have seen in those who deal with any kind of struggle in life, a tool that is used to handle and deal with this struggle. It is the attempt and eventual success of trying to see the good in the struggle. One attempts to identify the pieces or results of the struggle that are good, that are beneficial. Does it make the struggle disappear? No. Yet I have found that this mentality helps to put the struggle into a better perspective, or at least a more palatable one.

In regards to this philosophy, several positive results stand out. As a result of my disability, I am an inherently sensitive man. I had very little choice but to be concerned for the struggles of others because I have relied so much on their concern for mine. My disability has given me the desire to see others' struggles and to help them to minimize them. I have learned to take my familiarity with pain and use it to empathize with others. My disability has taught me humility, at least in the physical sense. (My pride in regards to my personality is best described as full-blown). I have learned to appreciate strength through a perspective impossible to possess without a disability.

I must say that one of my favorite silver linings is what I call X-ray vision. Throughout my life with a disability, I have noticed a wide variety of reactions towards me. Those that stare and don't say a word, those that stare and say a word, those who are comfortable when I actually bring it up, those who are varying degrees of uncomfortable when I bring it up, and so on. Yet, the one common denominator that ties these various reactions together is that my disability allows me to see people's reactions. It allows me to see people's hearts. It allows me to see people's strengths and weakness in dealing with me. It allows me X-ray vision into one part of who they are. Once those around me become aware of my condition, be it stranger or friend, I am able to sense a bit about the character of that person, as if my disability were an instant X-ray into who they are. I have become better over the years at using that X-ray, as well. At first, it was like a new power I did not yet know how to use. For example, I used to judge a quiet response to my disclosure as a lack of concern or feeling about it. Yet, those quiet people are often the ones who later lend me assistance on a hike or similar challenge without using their words. It taught me that some people would rather show their support through action.

Enter Brandt Lewis, my shining example of the X-ray at work. In my later summers at Camp Ramblewood, when I was about seventeen or eighteen and now a counselor for the camp, I met Brandt Lewis. Brandt was also a counselor at Ramblewood. He was from Arizona and a truly interesting guy. Brandt was also a very good looking guy. And he was fully aware of this. As a result of being a good looking guy, Brandt was used to having his way with women. He was a player from start to finish. He was on his game all of the time, and after a few summers at Ramblewood, Brandt developed a reputation that was less than favorable. He was kind of a jerk. He very rarely spoke with sincerity, and he very rarely treated women (or men, for that matter) with a great deal of respect. Brandt was in it for Brandt, or so it would seem.

For whatever combination of reasons, I always got along with him. I liked Brandt. He made me laugh and I did the same in return, and I wasn't a woman, so he had very little reason to piss me off. By the last summer that Brandt and I were at camp together, he and I had talked a small amount about my disability. Nothing of major substance, but it is fair to say that he was aware of my condition.

Each night of camp, after the kids had gone to sleep, a quarter of the staff would stay back to look after them. That left three quarters of the staff free to go out to the local town bar and get drunk enough to forget we were childcare workers. When the kids were asleep, those who were bar-bound would gather and walk up to the parking lot together. It was dark at this point and to get to the parking lot, we had to walk up a long hill and cross a small field. The trick with this journey was crossing the small field. It was no more than about 200 yards across, but it was made of uneven ground, filled with craters and dips. And to make it really interesting, it was completely overgrown with tall grass, allowing no vision as to where the dips and holes were located. It was a disabled person's minefield. Let's just say that for a person with my condition, walking across that field in the dark was not my favorite thing to do. For the most part, I was still in the phase of my journey where I kept my fear and discomfort to myself. I didn't want to be seen as different. I would dread that field as it approached, and when the group would start walking across it, I would simply slow down a bit and take it at the most normal pace that my fear and feet could muster.

Except for the nights when Brandt and I were both part of the bar-bound crew. On those nights, it looked something like this: the group of about 25 staff would be walking up the hill and laughing, and when we got to the edge of the field, the group would keep walking at their pace, barely noticing that they had entered the pothole field of doom. Except that Brandt, each night that he was with the group, would always slow down a bit at the edge of the field, and subtly position himself about one foot ahead of me. He would never look back or speak a word, but he just walked ahead of me with his hand held out behind him. This guy, this player who had little respect for women, a guy most people had written off as a total asshole, was the one member of that whole group who never missed a chance to be my guide through that field. Most nights, we would walk across that field just fine. Me, uneasy, and Brandt with his hand behind him. But when I would stumble or my foot would land in one of those invisible holes, I would grab his hand to keep me from falling, and he would be right there for me. I don't think anyone else in the group ever noticed that this went on, but I did. I have never forgotten it. It is a glowing example of the X-ray factor.

As a result of my disability, I was able to see a side of Brandt, a side of his truest heart that most people never would have seen and probably wouldn't have thought existed. I was fortunate to have that vision of him. He is a good guy who made a lifelong impression on me. There have been countless others who have helped me in this way over the years, countless others who have lended me a hand or an ear without me ever having to ask for it. I use my X-ray vision in all of those moments to see into the true heart of people. And more times than not, I see only good things.

(That's me, bottom row, second from the left. And that's Brandt, bottom row, second from the right.)

The View From My Village

"I've learned that people will forget what you said, people will forget what you did, but people will never forget how you made them feel."

—Maya Angelou

Chapter 8

The View From My Village.

During the dreaming phase of this book, a good friend and I were talking about what else to include, besides my story and perspectives. The conversation came around to the idea of including the perspectives of those in my life—those who, at various periods and various angles, have shared my experience with this disability. So I made a list of those I considered to be the major players in this village of mine. I sent out a request to these fine friends and relatives to write in about their experience knowing me and my path with a disability. And write in, they did. I have grappled with ways to edit this chapter and ways to piece together the point, but the bottom line always came back to *let it be*. I think each person's point is made in the entirety of their response. Therefore, save a few minor pieces of editing, I have included the entries that people wrote, in their original form. It makes for both a longer chapter and a more profound one as well. A disability affects the person who has it, as well as those who love that person. The following is the affect and experiences of those who love me …

Name: Joel Leman
Years known Jonah: 4
Title of connection to Jonah: Mentee

"There's a place where music meets wisdom, a place where the heart of a man is told in poems and song. There is a spot on earth where a man's soul is as right as beauty's tree gasping in the wind. Imagine this marvelous land where your disability is your strength and the crippled in body meets the crippled in soul. This, my friend, is where the winds of love roar through the manes of lions, and this, my brother, is where you will find Jonah sitting, cross-legged on a stump, talking by way of his drum. Waiting. Waiting for you and for me."

Name: Marilyn Berger
Years known Jonah: 35(+9months)
Title of connection to Jonah: Mother

Jonah was born on March 15, 1972. I was 26 years old. It was the third happiest days of my life; the day I got married being the first and the day my daughter was born being the second.

I was a relatively healthy person except for the fact that I tripped frequently and I was unable to jump and run fast. These were not big problems in my life until the summer of 1974, when I noticed I could not pick my feet up to run at all, and I was tripping most of the time.

After a visit to my podiatrist and an appointment with a neurologist, it was suggested I enter the National Institutes of Health for a full evaluation and proper diagnosing. The doctors explained to me I had a neurological disease called Charcot Marie Tooth, Disease or peroneal muscular atrophy. I now had a reason for the weakness I was experiencing, and I learned that this disease was hereditary.

My entire family was tested (mother, father, sisters, aunts and uncles). The disease came from my mother's side of the family. My mother had suffered with painful and weak feet and hands most of her adult life. She now had a reason for her weakness and felt so much guilt for giving this disease to me. I then had to deal with the fact that my children might have inherited CMT. I made the decision not to beat myself up over something I did not know I had when my daughter and son were conceived.

They say mothers have a natural intuitive instinct regarding their children. I had a strong feeling from the time I was diagnosed that Erica had not inherited CMT but Jonah had. I was correct on both counts. Jonah was tested when he was five years old and that began a journey for me and for Jonah, both physically and psychologically.

The physical aspects of the disease for me were addressed with short leg braces when I was 35 years old. Jonah was not physically ready for braces until he was 16, but he was not ready emotionally until several years later. That was the first struggle for me because I knew how the braces would help his walk, but I could not make this decision for him. I had to wait until he was ready.

At the beginning of each school year I met with Jonah's regular and physical education teachers along with Jonah. It was always important to me that they understand his disease and how it affected him. I also wanted to be sure he did not use his disability as an excuse not to participate. The physical education teacher in elementary school was wonderful at not singling Jonah out when he could not do something but instead found what Jonah could do and accentuated that. Jonah formed a close bond with this teacher and he became a strong role model in his early years.

The physical education teachers in junior and senior high school were also extremely appreciative of the education I provided them and were very willing to work with Jonah. They knew most sports were a frustration for him so they asked him to be a score keeper instead of a player. I really feel these early years enabled Jonah not to feel so different physically and also allowed him to embrace his disability in a more positive way. Jonah's charm and ease with people made him stand out as a natural leader and that is what we all tried to develop in him.

Starting at the age of seven years old, Jonah spent his summers at an overnight camp where he developed very close friendships. These friends were among the first ones he would open up to about his disease and his concerns about his disabilities. At camp, as in school, Jonah was always accepted for what he could do and not for what he could not do. His leadership skills, independence and feeling of self confidence blossomed during those summers away. It was very hard for me not to be with him all the time because I thought I needed to protect him from so many things. The truth is he did fine on his own.

I must add that from the time I was diagnosed I always looked at my disability as a minor problem in my life. I saw so many people who were dealing with so much more than I was. I know Jonah watched me and listened whenever I spoke of our disease to others. I wanted to be a strong and positive role model in his life so I decided the best thing I could do is teach by example. I continue to do that to this day.

Raising a child with a disability is a challenge but so is just raising a child. I always told Jonah the truth and always tried to respect his way of handling his disability even if I did not agree. We have always been able to discuss this subject openly and honestly. I think it was easier for me to handle the fears and uncertainties regarding my child having a disability because I was dealing with the very same problems and frustrations.

Jonah is now 35 and we still call each other when we are frustrated, when we have physical accomplishments to share and when we feel down because of the effect the disease has on our bodies. I also feel very strongly that the honest and caring friends and family members that Jonah has included in his life have made a big difference in his acceptance of his disease.

I am so proud of who Jonah is and how he deals with life. I know Jonah still watches how this disease affects my life physically and once again, I can only teach by example. I don't think I would have treated Jonah any differently if he was not born with CMT.

Name: Andrea Moore
Years known Jonah: 4
Title of connection to Jonah: Camp Colleague and Friend

I had no knowledge of Jonah's disability whatsoever until it was brought to my attention at camp. I had spent time with Jonah on a few occasions, including going out to dinner one-on-one, and nothing regarding his disability ever caught my attention at all. Later a staff member at the camp we both worked for mentioned that he wore braces on his legs, and I was surprised to hear that. The staff member was in turn surprised that I hadn't noticed and remarked that surely I had noticed how his hands are affected as well—I racked my memory, trying to recall if I had pictured anything different about his hands. We had spoken for hours at dinner, gesticulating frequently, and I had not noticed anything atypical about his hands, his ability to walk … in essence, I had not perceived a disability.

When Jonah and I next saw each other I imagined he would be a misshapen, hunchbacked creature like the Penguin from the Batman movie, and that somehow this had escaped my attention on our first meetings. But lo and behold, Jonah and I got together again and he remained as I remembered: entirely able-bodied. Upon closer inspection I did notice a slight stiffness in his gait due to the braces (hidden under his jeans), and I could discern a similar stiffness in his fingers, but nothing whatsoever that demanded more attention than the radiance of his personality.

It has been my experience that Jonah's "disability" is more of a diagnostic fact than a practical reality. As his friend I only ever remember that he experiences CMT when he asks me to help with tiny favors like buttoning a shirt button or taking the plastic from a straw on a box of juice. Actually, at the camp we worked for it seemed to me that Jonah's "disability" actually gave him the unique ability to reach out to others and develop understanding among groups of people. Children adore him and adults respect him, and in my estimation he has gained confidence, strength, and uncommon ability from his experience as a man "disabled."

Name: Julie Bass
Years known Jonah: 6
Title of connection to Jonah: Friend. Ex-Coworker turned employee. Only true "Hand Fan". Official birthday gift un-wrapper. We 'kind-of' dated for a while.

I guess I've never thought of how Jonah's condition really affects ME. In all actuality, it doesn't. When I think of my friend, or picture him in my head, my thoughts never land on his leg braces. I think of his smile, his agreeable laughter, his kind heart. Really, I don't see it as a 'disability'.

I remember when I started working with him he was just this guy that walked a little funny. I honestly can't remember when I discovered that he wore leg braces, nor can I remember when I found out why, for that matter. Somehow, we became friends. He is (by-the-way) one of the best huggers I have ever found, and soon enough our hugs became a huge dramatic production.

I will tell you this, however, and I know it sounds weird: I love his hands. He has the most beautiful, ahem, MANLY hands I have ever seen. It is something about the way that they are shaped, their definition. I used to always watch them in action, the way that they would delicately cradle objects. I suppose though, I still watch them and probably always will. There are times that I can recall watching … He has struggled to pick things up, or to open something. When I offer help, Jonah gladly hands over the task or will maybe give it a few more tries. The humbling thing is, he is okay with accepting help. And I am so glad to provide it. One particular time, at his birthday party, he was so caught up in conversation with his many friends that opening all of his gifts was too large a task. I had the honor of opening his gifts for him. What a rare delight that was! Any time, though, I'm there for him. Gift, mail, banana, whatever!

Name: Steve Weiss
Years known Jonah: Lifelong
Title of connection to Jonah: Cousin, friend, Possessor of CMT as well.

In all seriousness, Jo, I don't think either of us would be leading such productive and active lives without having had the understanding, support, inspiration, and motivation of the other. We are different people who have had varying experiences in life, but we have an unbreakable bond that in some ways connects us more closely than the best of friends.

As for you, I've seen you at various levels of comfort with your physical abilities, but you have inspired me throughout our lives with your willingness to involve others in your struggle with CMT. And I am in awe of how constructively you now confront your condition and the challenges you face. You have taught me an invaluable lesson—that one must first accept his limitations if he is to overcome them. Godspeed.

Name: Marc Ronick
Years known Jonah: 20
Title of connection to Jonah: Best Friend.

Jonah Berger **deals** with Charcot-Marie-Tooth disease, a type of Muscular Dystrophy. I refuse to say that Jonah **has** this disease. No, not because I'm in denial nor is he. Some people have a disease or a disorder and that disease has them. But that's not the case with Jonah. He truly deals with CMT as it comes. He doesn't flinch at the challenges. He doesn't complain about them. He faces them head on and pushes through them.

Everyone just assumes that it would be easy for me, Jonah's closest friend, his "brother", to write page after page about his battle with CMT. After all it's been a part of our friendship for 20 years. But it's not easy at all and it isn't because it's emotional for me to discuss. You see, through all of the years together, through all of the ups and downs that life brings, you might be surprised to hear that CMT has been one of life's challenges that I often forget he even has it at all. Surprisingly, it's something that we have only casually discussed sporadically throughout most of our friendship. It's very matter of fact for the both of us. We as brothers have accepted this for what it is and don't dwell on the negative.

Other people in my life will occasionally ask me, "So how's Jonah been?" 9 times out of 10 I can expect the following question to be "how's his MD?" It's a hard question to answer. "Its fine ... he's fine." How can it be any other answer? The disease itself has been getting worse but that's not the right answer to the question. The guy climbs mountains, hikes long trails, rows across rivers, and bikes across the state of Iowa! How do you think he's doing?

About 6 years ago, a large group of friends got together for a camping trip in Colorado Springs, Colorado. One day while we were there, Jonah kept insisting on gathering up the troops to hike up a mountain not far from our camp. He put together a group of 6 to 8 of us and off we went. At first, I thought very little of what a terribly difficult feat climbing up a mountain would be for him. That wasn't me being inconsiderate. It was because Jonah <u>deals</u> with CMT.

So after a short hike, we reached the mountain we'd decided we would take on. I looked up at this beast and my heart started racing. It was not the best time to discover that I'm afraid of heights. But I was there and we were all ready to head up that mountain, so I had to take a deep breath and we were off. It was then that I realized that Jonah faced a lot more than a fear of heights. But there he was with his giant walking staff in hand with no visible concerns about what he was about to embark on. It was amazing to watch him fight through each step. There were points along the way that each one of us lent him a helping hand but his determination was his most powerful assistant.

As we approached the half way mark, one of us couldn't go on any further. Most people would expect that it was the guy with CMT. Nope. It was the guy with his new-found fear of heights. What started as some heart pounding grew to shortness of breath and sheer terror. I could not go on. This was a huge moment for me. It was the first time after all of the years that I've known him that I truly came to grips with what Jonah was dealing with and how difficult it must be. It kept me going up that mountain more than I would have had he not been there but nonetheless I gave up. As I carefully walked down that mountain I couldn't have felt worse about myself. I couldn't believe a human being with full functionality of his legs couldn't get past a silly fear while one with a disease that causes weakness and wasting of the muscles and some loss of sensations to the feet and lower legs, treks forward with no sign of turning back.

I reached the bottom of the mountain defeated and watched Jonah and our friends reach the top. Wow. He did it. I was so proud of him. Then I realized that only half the challenge was completed. Heading down the mountain was going to be just as difficult if not more. But after a short breather at the top, there he was, at it again, headed back down. I watched each and every step in amazement continuing to be so proud of him. Obviously the rest of our crew made it down before him but always checked back to make sure he was doing okay. Of course he was. There was no reason to believe otherwise.

We were all at the bottom now and a few strangers made their way over. We struck up a conversation with them and suddenly Jonah had a built in audience cheering him on. He was in the final decent of his journey now, sweaty from his hard work, walking staff in hand, when one of the strangers called out, "He looks like Moses!" We all laughed in hysterics. He did look like Moses, and how suiting of an analogy it was. Here was this Jewish man walking down the mountain after a long journey, inspired and motivated, with a clear message of hope, strength and promise. It was quite poetic, really.

This is not to say that Jonah is able to do anything that anyone without this disease can do. The simple things to me can be some of the most difficult for him. Buttoning a button, tying a shoe lace, opening a jar of pasta sauce has become harder as each day goes on. But the point is that he finds a way. He doesn't get down about it. He doesn't accept defeat. He pushes through the challenge, big or small until it gets it done. We all should be so lucky to have Jonah's determination. No, we should all be inspired to have it. It has certainly been an inspiration for me in my life and although I haven't had a chance to face that fear of heights since that day, it will be impossible for me to back down from it, learning what I have from one of my very best friends.

Name: Lisa Runyon
Years known Jonah: 15
Title of connection to Jonah: Dear Friend. College and beyond....

When I think of Jonah, I simply think of my friend. The guy I have spent countless hours with: talking, laughing, going to class, practicing plays, filming, going on tour for the children's shows, eating family dinners, comforting, camping, and in general, just chillin'. Jonah's disability never comes to my mind when I think of Jonah. I think of his heart, his humor, his ability to make me laugh; I think that he is a quality person and really fun to be around. His disability is just a part of who Jonah is, just like his hair (or what's left of it) is dark brown, and he always drives a Jeep. I know that Jonah's disability is there, just like I know he is a boy and I know he is Jewish. However, his disability is not something that defines him. First and foremost, he is Jonah: my friend, a musician, a teacher, a good soul.

He has worn the leg braces since I've known him. However, there has never really been anything that his disability has limited him from doing. I know that there are things that are difficult for Jonah to do, such as buttoning a shirt without this helpful tool he has or opening a can of beer, I mean … soda. But there's a comfort of old friends, much like an older married couple. I know what may be difficult for him to do with his hands, and I just do it for him. We've shared hotel rooms when we've attended our friends' weddings, and when he's getting dressed, I may just go and button his shirt for him. Once when our crew of friends were camping, we wanted to go into the water and cool off. Okay … we were skinny-dipping on the private property of another of our friends. Jonah removed his leg braces to enter the water, was naked, and I exited the cover of water, naked, to help Jonah in. He leaned on my shoulder for support to get in the river. It's like the song, "Lean on me, when you're not strong 'cause I'll be your friend, I'll help you carry on …"

I feel like our whole circle of friends is like this. Support is given, the help that is needed, is given, and we don't focus on that. We simply help each other. Some of us have needed help in other ways, and that help is given. We see who needs what, and as a friend, we give that if we can. In the case of Jonah's disability, the helping hand he needs from time to time is nothing to me. I'm only helping a friend out the same way I help another friend by taking care of her pets when she's out of town.

In all the years I have known Jonah; I have never seen him let his disability control him, his mood, and his mind. It is there. It continues to progress. Things he could once do, he no longer can. Jonah knows this, and he knows it will continue to progress. However, since I have been his friend, he has, not even once, let his disability stop him from doing what he wanted to do. Jonah is amazing! He is strong, especially in his will, and I believe he can do anything. He has a disability. The disability does not have him.

Name: The Farwells
Years known Jonah: 3
Title of connection to Jonah: Clients and friends.

I think of Jonah in many ways and on many levels. He is mentor to our 13 year old son, Ryan. Like Jonah, Ry also has Muscular Dystrophy. They travel our city together exploring restaurants, music stores, museums, parks or whatever fantastic place grabs their fancy. With Jonah, both Ryan and I share a deep understanding, trust and joy. Jonah understands the level of pain and frustration that Ryan feels when he falls or when he is too scared to ask for simple help. He understands the path that Ry may physically take and has openly discussed leg braces with him. Ryan quickly shuns this conversation, and Jonah admits that he did too at Ryan's age. Personally I trust Jonah to know when he can push Ry or just let him be. For Ryan, I think that Jonah is pure fun—banging on drums together or singing at the top of their lungs inside a car. They share a sense of humor and a zest for life which is the basis of this wonderful, many tiered friendship.

Name: Becky Palmisano
Years known Jonah: 12
Title of connection to Jonah: Ex-girlfriend/dear friend.

Let it Bee.... Actually, I never realized Jonah had a disability. It was maybe a couple of years into our friendship that I realized it. I can't recall how it came up, but I think at some point I asked a mutual friend, "Does Jonah wear braces?" Their response was probably something like, "um, yeah, I guess so," and, well, that was the last time I thought of it for some time.

None of us ever knew Jonah for his "braces." Nope. Back in the day we were a solid group of friends. We cared for people because they cared for us. We cared, not what they looked like or how they were able to navigate their bodies around the world, but for how they behaved and how they treated each of us as individuals. Jonah was no exception.

While the knowledge of Jonah's braces had minimal impact on my day to day interaction with him, to some degree I suppose my thoughts shifted. I probably spent some days "feeling out" his disability—finding myself perhaps a bit curious about what it was, what it does to him, and how it debilitated him or how he felt about it. I didn't know too much. I think I just knew it was MD. On the surface … you couldn't tell, really. The only times I remembered him struggling around was on an occasional hike. I remember crossing creeks and climbing hills with Jonah. I remember him pushing forward without too much effort or without overt thought. I remember wanting to go back and check on him, and perhaps sometimes I floated back to say hi, but never to offer assistance. He seemed to have his abilities under control and didn't need any extra help. Not knowing how he felt about his disability, I never openly offered help. I wasn't sure if that would be something he wanted. So, on those occasions I simply offered my presence—not really just for checking in on how he was getting along, but probably because more so … I just plain liked Jonah. He was good for me and comfortable to be around.

We got attacked by bees once. That sucked. We were hiking and attacked by a big swarm of bees. I remember running, yelling "f**k, f**k" and not knowing where Jonah was or how to get back to him. I knew he was getting attacked, too, and I knew he couldn't run as quickly. In retrospect, running didn't really help to get the bees off. I remember thinking afterwards how it sucked that I could run and he couldn't. Yet in the end, we both had about the same amount of stings. So really, his ability to run neither helped nor hindered the situation. It just was. It's a fond memory.

Somehow over the years I fell in love with Jonah. His disability never crossed my mind. Being with him wasn't always easy, but it had nothing to do with his disability. But being with him was probably one of the closest experiences to another person that I've ever had. During these days I learned more about Charcot Marie Tooth disease. I learned what it was, and how it affected his body. I learned about the family and the range of the disease. I learned that he could perhaps pass it on to a child.

My family met Jonah. They loved him. He was kind. He was friendly. He was handsome. He was thoughtful. And one time a family member said to me, "but Becky, it would be a lifetime of difficulty and pain." They felt that as his disease progressed, he would become more debilitated and with that came great responsibility and patience. I remember thinking about this. I asked him more questions. I read more about CMT. I just couldn't find it in me to say that even if this man needed to be pushed around in a wheelchair at some point that it wouldn't be worth the amount of love that I had for him or him for me. I didn't see how this "pain" of caring for a disabled loved one outweighed the tremendous benefits of the relationship. So I moved on with minimal thought towards my family member's concern.

I loved this man. Part of this love was expressed through my efforts to support him with his disability. I talked with him about it. I rubbed his feet and hands. I was curious, concerned and comfortable with it. And it occupied maybe 10% of our total time together. It was not what brought us closer. It was not what drew us apart. It just was.

If ever there was a moment where I found myself selfishly concerned about Jonah's CMT, it was when I thought that we might start a family together. I started thinking about the chances of a child having CMT. On one hand, here is Jonah with a productive, active life. So bringing a child into the world with CMT couldn't possibly be a bad thing. Then again, Jonah spoke about painful days growing up with a disability and learning how to deal with being different. So I thought about the pain that a child might experience while growing up. Jonah also spoke about how his mother, who also has CMT, was his pillar of strength during these days. So a strong family could certainly provide a strong support both physically and emotionally for a child dealing with confusion or insecurity around a disability.

I think what concerned me more was money. Yes. Every few years Jonah got new braces. They were expensive. There would be a cost to raising a child with CMT. I myself wasn't even insured at the time. Jonah wasn't either. I remember asking myself, "How would we raise a child with a disability when we can't even find a job that gives even ME insurance?" Could we afford that? Was that fair?

These thoughts never influenced my decision on whether or not to be with him. These were thoughts and concerns that never actually hit the table. Our relationship ended for other reasons. We never made it to this stage of decision-making. Seven years later we are still friends. Perhaps we aren't as close as we used to be. Distance on many levels has separated our day-to-day. Yet, we are friends, nonetheless. To this day, I still find great joy in finding him lotions that he likes to keep his hands from being dry. Or socks that are thin, breathable, that would help protect his skin from the rub of the braces. I'm still curious about what new braces he wears, how they work and what type of side effects they cause. I'm still curious because I still care. I would still rub his hands or feet in a heartbeat if that's what he wanted. Because I can.

Jonah B. has many faults. As do I. As do you. But never would I consider one of these faults to be his disability. If nothing else, it is strength, a strength that provides him with focus and with great empathy for learning about and including individuals with a range of differences in his life. It is a strength that provides direction for his heart and direction for his profession. Without CMT, Jonah would not be who he is. And that would be a great loss!

Name: John Gladbach (Horus)
Years known Jonah: 6
Title of connection to Jonah: Colleague, Friend, Co-Adventurer.

    Jonah, you have been a good friend to me for these past four years and though we have not known each other very long, I feel we have so much in common that has allowed us to become quick and dear friends. It wouldn't appear at first glance that we have much in common. We grew up in different parts of the country. Our religious upbringing is different. I am from a large family; you have one sibling. I guess our shared sense of humor, our curiosity and love of the road, our common calling to work with kids and our love of a good campfire are more than enough to keep a corn-fed Midwest German boy and Maryland Jew talking for years.

    Your disability is another example of how you and I are different, but I have learned that in the things we do physically we are mostly the same as well. As a kid, my attitudes about people with disabilities were, at best, patronizing. As a teacher, I have been to a number of high school graduations and have witnessed the inevitable standing ovation for "the kid in the wheelchair." It happened at my own graduation. A student who had been paralyzed playing football our sophomore year got a 1-minute ovation as he crossed the stage to receive his diploma. I stood, too, and got goose bumps thinking of the heroic effort he had displayed. I spoke to him a few years later and recalled that day.

    "Yeah, that was embarrassing," he confessed.
    I was puzzled.

"What did I do?" he asked. "I graduated from high school. So did everyone else. It was just another reminder that I was different. I don't want to be anyone's mascot and I don't want people to make a big deal out of me doing things that I am fully capable of doing." It was when I met you that this lesson finally sank in. I mostly didn't notice that you were different and generally forgot, anyway. Mostly you and I are the same. I guess that hike in Utah really made me realize one of the ways our lives are different.

We left the car in the late afternoon, climbing gradually up the slick rock stone in the desert heat. We were all excited to get to Delicate Arch for sundown. We skirted the rim of the basin that was crowned with the impressive arch, tiptoed around the front and made our way out to a tongue of land behind the arch. We took our time, careful not to slide down the slope of the immense bowl or off the sheer rock cliff to our left.

We sat at the edge of a precipice, listened to the wind and played drum and flute as the rocks glowed with the warm orange and pink of sunset.

As the light faded, someone had the sense to rouse us from our hypnotic calm. "Guys, we better get off this cliff before it gets too dark to see."

The way down is always more dangerous. We were tired, our enthusiasm for the summit was doused and we now had to make our way back over the steep and precarious slope we had picked our way across earlier.

This time was not nearly as fun. Each step had to be carefully calculated. Handholds were difficult to judge now that we were enveloped in near total darkness. My legs were shaking as my toes clung perilously to the tiniest of cracks in the wall. Below me were fifty feet of steep sandstone and then a drop to the valley floor. At one point I had to sprawl flat against the rock, spread-eagle, to stop my slide. My face, belly and arms felt as if someone had used an electric sander on them, but I was safe. I finally crested the hump right in the center of the arch and made my way to the safety of the mesa top. I was scared but I had done it. I had challenged myself and had made it! I hunched over, lungs heaving, as I struggled to catch my breath.

My friends were having a little harder go of it.

Below me, Chad and Jonah were stuck. They were carefully surveying the wall for a safe foothold, taking their time where I had foolishly bolted up steep angles, hoping my tread would grip the rough stone.

"Come on, guys," I shouted down to them. "We got to get out of here and get down this mountain". I was growing impatient and wondering why they were taking the long way around a boulder, skirting it from below.

"Come on guys, just go for it. Use your legs to push you up and grab the handhold on your left."

They didn't seem to be interested in taking the quicker route. I was puzzled by their choice to take the longer, harder path.

Chad reached me and we waited, still breathing hard, for Jonah, who was making his way up a crevice behind the boulder.

"What the hell is taking him so long?" I asked impatiently.
"He's coming, Horus," Chad assured me.
"Yeah, but by why didn't he just come up the way I did?"
"You weren't walking with braces on your legs, Horus."
The look of surprise on my face must have been amusing.
I had simply forgotten.

I had forgotten that my friend's brain has difficulty moving the joints in his wrists and ankles. I had forgotten that my friend walks everywhere with plastic braces that reach from his calf to his toes and reinforce the angle formed where the foot meets the leg. I had forgotten that he lugs those things around with him everywhere he goes and that far from being a burden to him, they offer him freedom. Freedom to do physically anything within the bounds of the limits he chooses.

I had struggled up that rock. Jonah had struggled up that rock. I had carefully chosen the route best suited for my strengths and skills. So had Jonah. I had subjected myself to considerable danger and effort for the thrill of summiting that beautiful mesa and seeing that gorgeous sunset. We all had and though it was difficult, it was well worth the effort.

A man in wheelchair once asked me if I wished I could fly. I admitted that this was one of my favorite daydreams since childhood. He got me to admit, however, that I wasn't miserable because I could not fly, that I didn't sit around, lamenting my life and what could have been if only I had been born with wings.

"Besides, you can walk a lot better than a bird can," he assured me.

There are some things I can do with my body that Jonah cannot. There are many things that others can do that I cannot. Mostly, Jonah, like any other person, does what he can and when he can't do it the way everyone else does, he does it a different way. It may take more time, he may pick his way around the rocks differently than most, but he makes it up the mountain just the same.

Jonah crested the lip of the summit to find Chad and I, hands on knees, still struggling to catch our breath.

"Damn, that was hard," Jonah gasped.

"I know," I replied.

"Nice work, brother," he said as he congratulated Chad with a high-five and patted me on the back.

"Now let's get down this mountain," Jonah said. "I need some macaroni and cheese."

✦

Name: Jason Griffin
Years known Jonah: 6 months
Title of connection to Jonah: Leg brace technician, friend. "Blood, sweat, and tears."

What can I say about a man like Jonah? Jonah has been interesting to work with, to say the least, mainly because of his lifestyle and his expectations. He is an unbelievably active person and refuses to live any other way. His activity level has genuinely pushed the envelope for the braces that he uses. We have had many different types of AFO (ankle foot orthotic), several of which have really been experimental. His size, strength, activity level, and determination have caused us to think outside the box. Most people with his condition just do not put the same severe abuse on their braces that Jonah does on a daily basis. He has managed to break just about everything we have managed to fabricate for him. His persistence to fabricate the type of braces he needs to be as active as he is, especially in lieu of the fact that they do not exist, is impressive. I think most orthotists would be frustrated with his determination; I on the other hand am thrilled with his positive outlook. We have tried and are still trying to satisfy his expectations as well as we can. The idea that he has managed to hike, bicycle, and exert himself in his condition demands respect and admiration. He is a positive influence to anyone who is willing to listen to his heroic story. I am thrilled to be able to work with him and I look forward to many years of helping him climb the next mountain he charges up! More than that I am proud to call Jonah my friend!

Name: Chad Bouchard
Years known Jonah: 7
Title of connection to Jonah: Friend, co-worker, canoe mates.

Jonah was a groomsman in my wedding a few years ago, and a few days prior to the ceremony we went to get the tuxedos fitted. All of the groomsmen and myself met at the tuxedo store for the official fitting and upon our arrival we were given a hanger containing all of the various tuxedo components and were told to find a dressing room and to try it all on. While I was in my dressing room putting on the various layers of clothing, I heard Jonah laugh. Jonah was supposed to be assembling the various parts of the tuxedo, like the rest of us. Following the laugh, Jonah asked if the tuxedo came with a girlfriend to help him put it on. After no response, I heard Jonah call for help and walk out of his dressing room. The shirt was on, but not buttoned and in one hand was his tie and in the other was his vest. An employee was now waiting by the dressing rooms and greeted Jonah upon his exit with the excess gear in tow. He asked the employee if she could help him finish assembling his tuxedo, he explained that due to his physical condition he was not able to physically dress himself in the tuxedo attire. Moments like that would make some people feel awkward, but for Jonah it's become a way of life. Some people might have been too shy or ashamed to ask a complete stranger to help dress them, however, the request is part of Jonah's reality.

Jonah is one of the most positive people I know and from his perspective every cloud has a silver lining. When we spend time together and things are frustrating or the results aren't what we hoped for, Jonah gladly provides a smile. He is quick to point out the outcomes that could be worse, and how fortunate we are in the big picture. Living with MD constantly creates challenges that force creative problem solving and positive approaches for Jonah. His positive outlook helps put my life into perspective. I am a physically sound individual, and when I am complaining about some trivial situation I am forced to focus on what I can control. I, like Jonah, am learning not to get caught up with things out of my control and instead celebrate and enjoy the things that are within my control.

✦

Name: Dave Cowan (The Unbalanced Force)
Years known Jonah: 5
Title of connection to Jonah: Friend, Biking Instructor, Colleague, a true unbalanced force

Newton's First Law as Applied to Jonah: Jonah at rest tends to stay at rest and Jonah in motion tends to stay in motion with the same speed and in the same direction unless acted upon by an unbalanced force.

As I'm sure many have already commented, my experience with Jonah's disability has been more beneficial for me than for him. I've had the unique opportunity to watch Jonah's struggle with his disability from many different angles, some of which are more scenic than others.

There is the Jonah amongst his friends, who although jokingly protests that his disability prevents him from washing dishes, cleaning up, or completing any other menial task, he takes on every opportunity to demonstrate that he is equally capable as everyone else in the room. During the few times he isn't as capable, he has the trust and understanding to lean on these very people for assistance.

There is Jonah amongst his clients and campers, serving as the ultimate role model. With them he is outgoing, charismatic, and hilarious with a disability. In these moments, Jonah is a beacon to those fraught with overcoming the limitations (both physically, emotionally and socially imposed) of their own disability.

He provides a possibility and reminds them that it is viable to do or be something special, despite having a disability.

There is the Jonah alone that must wrestle with these same tumultuous waters. The Jonah that closes up for awhile, shields himself from the pain, and withdraws long enough to get a fresh breath of air so that he can continue showing the clients, campers, and friends that there are few, if any, truly insuperable challenges.

What I have learned, as a friend to Jonah, is actually something that I learned in a physics class many moons ago: Jonah at rest tends to stay at rest, while Jonah in motion tends to stay in motion unless acted upon by an unbalanced force. Perhaps the same characteristics that make him capable to deal with the day to day rigor of stepping into those braces every morning are the same characteristics that can create stumbling blocks for him. The same determination and resilience that helps him up the mountain are the very same characteristics that can prevent him from even trying to get out of bed. Without inspiration or drive he has the potential to "stay at rest," but properly motivated by "unbalanced forces," he has the amazing capability to charge forward, achieving the insurmountable with chutzpah.

As I said earlier, Jonah has taught me much more than I'll ever teach him. For example, I may provide the unbalanced force to encourage Jonah to get on a bicycle, but that is the easy part. The hard part is overcoming the fear of getting on a bicycle after 20 years. The hard part is learning how to adapt the bike and your body to the physical atrophy that has occurred since the last time a pedal turned. The hard part is knowing that the physically able will pedal harder, faster, and easier than you and being okay with that. The hard part is pushing yourself to get back on that bicycle day after day knowing that there are so many obstacles and so many naysayers that think that it isn't possible. The hard part is stepping into your braces every morning wondering what struggle you might face. Jonah's daily grapple with the hard part has been inspirational to me.

Next month Jonah will be pedaling 70 miles a day in debilitating heat across the barren state of Iowa. He will be demonstrating yet again his determination by "remaining in motion," through Newton's first law.

Name: Jill Manner
Years known Jonah: 12
Title of connection to Jonah:
Jonah: Jill/Six Million Dollar Man: Bionic Woman (coming to NBC this Fall!!!)

Blue skies, bright sun and 75 degree temperatures ... not bad for a June afternoon in the Big Apple but, still, I'm sweating my ass off. I've been walking the streets of SoHo for nearly 6 hours: stifling panic attacks when faced with the task of crossing a busy street before the blinking signal holds steady at solid red, fighting the crowds of strangers charging down uneven sidewalks, and struggling to stay upright when one of them runs into my shopping bags. The girls I'm with are ready to take a lunch break so they dart into a bistro on the corner and request a table. Though there are several vacant ones to choose from on the main level, the hostess grabs three menus and heads for a narrow spiral staircase in the corner ... fuck, this meal better be worth it. My shopping companions take the lead but are 4-5 steps up before realizing the difficulty this staircase poses to me. They turn and offer a hand but, at that point, I have gained momentum (with my shopping bags in one hand and a firm grip on the railing with the other), and I need to them keep moving. I feel frustrated, exhausted, and down-right angry with the laundry list of challenges this bustling urban environment has posed. Then the cosmos send me the sign I need to see the brighter side of the situation: a familiar face seated at the first table near the top ... it's Lowell (an old friend of Jonah's). No, I don't stop dead in my tracks to say "hi," but I think of a certain "Six Million Dollar Man" and am reminded that there ARE others out there who feel my pain. I wonder "WWJD?"—"What Would Jonah Do?" and the whole experience seems more comical than miserable.

I was born with a birth defect called spina bifida. This means that, during the first few weeks of my existence in utero, some force (perhaps my mother's chain smoking) interfered with my neurological development and my spinal column never completely closed. The level of severity varies from case to case so I am actually a fortunate one; since the opening occurred at the base of my spine, my spina bifida mildly affects my mobility and bladder/bowel function only. I walk with the help of a brace on my right leg and I pee through straws instead of on my own. Camping, a shared pastime amongst Jonah & friends, is always an interesting experience for me because, while hiking to and from a campsite WITH gear is never my strong suit, I can leave my mark on a tree as well as any man when it's time to relieve myself.

I remember noticing Jonah when I moved into Cambridge Hall for my freshman year of college in 1992. The dorm was the only fully ADA compliant building on campus ... therefore, it seemed like a logical dumping ground for every special needs student requesting on-campus housing. I also took notice of him when I was required to attend a campus production of "Harvey" for class credit. Jonah had a role in the show and, when he appeared on stage for the first time, I remember being intrigued by the fact that he'd chosen theater as his path given his physical limitations. It didn't even occur to me that MY insecurities might not be shared by EVERYONE with a disability. This became <u>revelational</u> later on.

Periodically, I get urges to reach out to the disabled population when insecurities or related health issues surface, so I've met my share of fellow "crips." It's rare to form real connections with those folks based on disability alone, though. When I met Jonah for the first time in 1995, however, I discovered that we had more than a dorm and distinct limp in common ... I was wowed by his sense of humor. With a slightly off-center sense of humor myself, I am always impressed that Jonah never fails to get the joke. Psychologists would say we've developed our cunning wit as a defense mechanism to detract attention away from our physical challenges ... I say life handed us lemons and we mixed up some wicked Long Island iced teas!

Earlier in life, I used to harbor such angst over the things my body couldn't do. With Jonah in my life, I've learned to appreciate the things that my body CAN do and to always try redefining my limits by pushing myself from time to time. I started teaching with anxiety over physically keeping up with my students, only to discover that a "look" can command respect better than any form could. I got pregnant and feared that my limitations would eventually threaten the safety of my baby, only to realize she's a much more tolerant and caring person because of them. My strength may never come from my body ... instead, I am driven by the energy of the people with whom I choose to surround myself. Jonah, with his heart full of love and his infectious laugh, is clearly someone whose presence makes me stronger.

In fact, my most memorable encounter with Jonah has to be our grueling hike up to Cunningham Falls. The word "hike" never conjured up negative connotations for me until that day. It started off harmless enough … a simple dirt path bordered by weathered landscape timbers, directing foot traffic up a gradual incline (step, drag, step, drag). Eventually the path included some landscape timbers turned perpendicular to form deep mezzanines as the grade increased (step, drag, step, drag, STRETCH, step, drag, step, drag, STRETCH). The trail was broken up occasionally by a fallen tree which required a little teamwork. With all other able-bodied friends miles ahead, Jonah & I were natural partners (step, drag, STRETCH, pull, stumble, step, drag). Things really started getting dicey when make-shift stairs around a series of exposed tree roots appeared along an even steeper incline (step, together, STRETCH, together, pull, wobble, balance, SWEET JESUS!). But, damned if that view of the fresh spring water cascading down the mountainside wasn't that much more spectacular knowing he and I were triumphant in our journey. I'm pretty sure I sweat my ass off that day, too.

❖

Name: Erica Berger (A.K.A.-Styx)
Years known Jonah: His whole life.
Title of connection to Jonah: Sister

I compare myself to my brother. Maybe all siblings compare themselves to their brothers and sisters, and notice what's the same and what's different. Jonah has my father's ability to lead a group, and my mother's heart. He can express his emotions well at almost any time and does so regularly. If you are in Jonah's life and you mean something to him, you know about it. He lets you know. I'm more like my father in matters of the heart, more cautious about expressing my feelings, and using my intellect to lead the way. Jonah is the mountain man; I'm the city girl. He puts on clothes that are comfortable; I put on what looks hip. He liked the lemon pie; I liked the chocolate cupcakes. On it goes. And then there is Charcot. By the random chance of the genetic lottery, he inherited Charcot and I did not. There was a 50/50 chance for each of us. He got it. I didn't. That one fact has had a tremendous impact on our lives.

This comparison is in some ways a gift. I appreciate what many take for granted. When I am tying my shoes or doing some kind of vigorous exercise, or skating, or walking on the beach, it occurs to me to be grateful that I can. I appreciate what my body can do in so many moments. I make an effort to use my body for all that it can do, because I know that is a privilege. The reality, however, is that this appreciation is mixed with guilt as I am ever aware that, for Jonah, some of what I can do is either not possible or much more difficult. It's a long standing debate for me, though maybe not one I talk about. Can I feel great about what I can do, without feeling bad about what Jonah can't? What kind of sister, person, friend, does that make me? Jonah lives in another state, and I don't see my mother every day. This means that there are stretches of time that I lose awareness of how it is progressing for both of them. Is that okay?

I had a special opportunity, as a social worker in New York, to run groups for siblings of children with disabilities. It was one of my first chances to share this debate with people who understood it well. With one of the groups—teenagers—we created a video by interviewing each of them about their experiences growing up with their siblings. They decided to interview me as well, to include me in the process they created. One by one, they spoke with a level of maturity and a depth of caring that I recognize in myself. One by one, they also cried and spoke in quieter tones about the more painful parts, about their guilt and about their worries. It was remarkable, mostly because it gave me a chance to consider that the maturity and caring might not have been a coincidence. It's possible that we share it because of the view we grew up with, knowing that health and ability are not a given.

Within my family, there was a precedent set. My mother was diagnosed with Charcot when I was a small child. While I was too young to remember what feelings went along with that diagnosis, I do have early memories of my father working at the Jerry Lewis Telethon every year. He would stay up all night and supervise the phones. Many other family members would join in the effort. It just became an adopted cause, and a priority. My mother was not a complainer; in fact, she was the opposite. She just didn't raise Charcot in discussions or focus on what she could not do. Though I can see the progression of it taking its toll, her attitude was one of handling what she has to handle and appreciating what she could do. When friends would meet her for the first time, and comment on her braces, it made me aware of how I had forgotten all about them. Not that I didn't see her put them on each day, but she didn't make them an issue. When Jonah began to show evidence of Charcot, in his walk, and in his hands, it was more of a mix. Jonah brought it up more often, sometimes joking with our cousin who has Charcot, too. Sometimes, Jonah brought it up because he is just the kind of guy who tells you what's going on for him. It was also different because I didn't know my mother at all of the ages I've known Jonah. I didn't see the evolution of the disease in the same way I have with my brother.

When I see Jonah again for the first time in a few months, it always strikes me. I feel pain when I watch him walk across a room without his braces on, when I watch him at the beach struggling with and then avoiding the sand. I feel it in a way that escapes words. Though there is always awareness that Charcot is mild by comparison to what other people have to deal with, and mild in the range of muscular dystrophy diseases, that's the rational part. The feelings part just hurts for him and wishes he didn't have to struggle with actions that take me a second to do. I don't necessarily say anything about it; in fact, usually I don't. But it rests with me. It is there.

What I feel most, however, more than appreciation, or guilt, is tremendous awe and respect. I have watched my brother, with amazement, as he has shaped his life in a way that incorporates the Charcot. In a very matter of fact way, he just simply found his passions in areas that Charcot could not mess with. He could not play sports in high school, but became the manager of the women's volleyball team, a position that set him up socially better than many jocks at his school. He formed friendships through the theater, in college, with a group that truly valued and accepted the spirit of another person, and minimized the material or physical aspects that are really just packaging anyway. He moved to Colorado, where his love of nature, and camping could grow. Jonah found the place where his desire to not flush the toilet much was the norm! He studied special education and formed a career that involved helping kids who have a range of disabilities. I can only imagine the power of his involvement in each of their lives. Above all, what Jonah can do is keep his eye on the ideal, on the way the world should be, and not accept less. In what way his disability helped to create that, I don't know. I do know that his perspective, and by association, mine, is different because of Charcot. One never knows what they are capable of until they are tested, and I hope that I would have handled Charcot as well as Jonah has and continues to do. But not knowing, I can honestly say that Jonah blows me away.

Name: Jason Conn
Years known Jonah: 20
Title of connection to Jonah: Old Friend

Jonah was my best friend during some very important and formative teenage years, though I suspect there are several others that would say the same.

I met Jonah around the age of 14 when I went to overnight camp at Camp Ramblewood in Western Maryland. I went with a couple of neighborhood friends that I had known for years, but quickly developed a close friendship with Jonah. He was a dynamic personality, even then.

Although Jonah didn't need or use braces or require any assistance then, I remember noticing that he didn't run like the rest of the kids. But it never stopped him from participating, and never (at least outwardly) changed his outlook on the summer fun.

It is this aspect of his personality that I respected so much. It was this that allowed me to feel comfortable enough to ask him about his about his disability, and how it affected him. He never shied away, or changed the subject like most would do. He was open and honest about both the physical and social challenges he faced.

If you can imagine a couple of 14 year old boys sitting and talking about life in this way—it's a lot to comprehend. At a time in life that adolescent boys are trying to establish their manhood, we cried together.

Jonah says this was a very important moment for him. It enabled him to talk openly and confidently about his disability, to express his feelings and to not be ashamed. It means a lot to me to think that I made an impact on Jonah's life, as he has dedicated his life to helping so many others.

This was the beginning of an incredible friendship. Jonah opened his home and family to me. I'll never forget participating in the Jerry Lewis Telethon with the Bergers. But of course most of our friendship was built around standard teenage stuff—girls, friends and parties.

While life has moved us far apart in distance, and we don't speak quite as often as we did, Jonah will always be a brother to me. I learned so much from Jonah about what it means to be a friend. In many respects there is nothing more important in life.

✦

Name: James Weise
Years known Jonah: 4
Title of connection to Jonah: Giddy school children stuck in men's frames.

After camp is over I park the car far away from a trailhead. I know Colorado well and know where I can scramble my way up to 12,000 ft, just to be alone. I breathe hard and sweat, but otherwise my "able" body glides over rock faces, through rushing streams, and under half fallen trees. I hike in the high mountain because this allows me space to think, and today I think of my friend Jonah. I am sad because Jonah can't join me on this kind of excursion. He is disabled.

Step back a moment. I don't think of Jonah as being "disabled." This is not to diminish Jonah's genuine struggles with CMT. To a fair degree, I am aware of how his illness affects him. But I prefer to define people (when I do) by their abilities, not by their dis-abilities.

Jonah and I met at camp. This camp is designed to bring intensive therapy, new experiences and adventure to children. Specifically, this camp is for children who have significant to severe delays; mentally and/or physically. While addressing their handicaps, we see these kids for who they are and what they can be. We highlight their strengths and work to increase their abilities.

Here, at camp, I have learned much from Jonah. In the camp setting Jonah is a dynamic counselor, and an administrator. He is responsible for planning, organizing and motivating these kids to reach beyond their maximum goals. These campers look to Jonah for guidance, reassurance, and hugs. On day one of camp I watched while Jonah set up the large equipment in the therapy rooms, reorganized a week's worth of food for five dozen people, confirmed Thursday's river rafting launch times, nursed a camper's small wound, introduced new campers to each other, and delegated a hundred other chores to a dozen staff members. Disabled?! Please.

Then, later in the week, I saw Jonah step out of a swimming pool. He doesn't have his leg braces on and without this simple aid I see that every step requires significant effort. Without pants to camouflage, I can now see that below the knees, his legs have no definition. The calf muscles are emaciated. In that instant my impulse is to run over and support him under his arms, carry him to his destination. Surely he needs someone's assistance to walk across the room. As a therapist, that is what I am trained to do, help people in need. Naturally, he manages to get to the locker room, without my charity.

Continuing my mountain-top thoughts ... Earlier that week I remember the joy and laughter of Jonah entertaining the troops. Much to my envy, Jonah can bang out complex rhythms on his Djembe drum. He can quickly change the time signature, stop time, or double up the beats, he adds to the music a rich tenor singing voice and well-timed comedic shtick. Now Jonah and I both share a love—nay, passion, for music. But he can *create* music. Me? I long ago gave up in my efforts to learn to play an instrument. Sure, I can bend my fingers into a chord, I can bang on the skin of a drum, but "music" is not an accurate description of the noise I make. I have learned that with the support and aid of say, a large drum circle, I can bang away with great joy and enthusiasm. Immersion in an orchestra of dependable rhythm makers helps me to keep my hands in time, and the sheer volume hides my stray, lost beats. I am a part of the band, if only because of intensive assistance. Without this assistance I cannot make music.

But not being able to create music is not how I define myself. And "disabled" is certainly not how I define Jonah.

Name: Tami D'Amico
Years known Jonah: 5
Title of connection to Jonah: Friend, ex-girlfriend, a cooling breeze....

Jonah has shown me that despite physical limitation one can and should focus energy upon things that deserve it. His CMT may have prevented us from skiing great mountains together, but it never stopped us from exchanging great words of wisdom. One night we had to wait a long time for a table at a restaurant and I remember being worried that there was no place for us to sit down while we waited. You see, I had assumed that Jonah needed to sit down because he had braces on his legs. I didn't know Jonah well back then, but I quickly discovered that he was not about to let his disability get in the way of a fine evening. We walked around the block several times while we waited for our table, and I'm certain that it was I who tripped on the uneven sidewalk far more often than he. This was the first of many long valuable conversations to come. I have learned much from his creative mind and poetic sense of seeing the world around him. He has taught me to see beyond a person's physical being and to look deeper into their heart embracing each other's similarities, but even more so finding inspiration in our differences. I remember a night when Jonah stumbled a little bit and I put my hand out to grab hold of him, saying don't worry I'll catch you. He may have needed the stability of my physical strength on that night, but there was a time that it was his inner strength that kept me from falling a far greater distance. There is a peace about Jonah that is engraved upon my heart. I know that CMT has challenged him, caused him pain, and I'm certain created great frustration for him at times. I am humbled and inspired by the way he chooses to project peace and compassion towards others as opposed to bitterness and defeat. It has always been easy to see beyond Jonah's disability because I know with all my heart that he is seeing beyond and looking deeper within me.

Name: Marty Berger
Years known Jonah: His Lifetime
Title of connection to Jonah: Father, teacher.

Men have many expectations as they enter into marriage and ultimately into fatherhood. I was no different than most. I looked forward to setting up housekeeping with my wife and overtly accepting the responsibilities of a husband. On December 27, 1966, with a combined income of $8,000.00, the Marty and Marilyn Berger family was born. Oh, what fun. New jobs, new car, new apartment, new experiences on a daily basis learning to care about and for one another. Then, in January of 1969, we were pregnant and in September we were parents of Erica. Wow! I was a father. What a kick. I drove home from the hospital yelling out the window, "I'm a father." What could possibly beat this feeling of pride and happiness? A gorgeous, healthy girl. We were a "family."

Then, August of 1971 we were pregnant again and March 15, 1972 Jonah arrived. It would be dishonest not to admit that I had hoped for a boy. Every father, as much as they love their daughters, deep down inside, hopes for a son. Carry on the family name, toss a football around, go to a baseball game, roughhouse; all the stereotypical macho-boy stuff. Wonderful to have a daughter, amazing to have a son.

In 1974 Marilyn was diagnosed with Charcot Marie Tooth disease, a diagnosis that explains the high gait with which she walks and the propensity for tripping with which she has lived her life. We were terrified by the knowledge that it is a progressive disorder which could take one's ability to walk and that it may very well have been passed to Erica and Jonah. We spent the next five years coming to grips with Marilyn's braces, a chore which she handled far better than I. I had a very difficult time recognizing Marilyn's need to be independent. It also took me a while to realize that her desire to do things for herself was not a rejection of my ever-present willingness to help, but rather her developing strength which would serve her well throughout her lifetime.

In 1979 we finally had Jonah tested. We had both watched the kids developing and had noticed Jonah's high gait and his frequent tripping. Erica displayed no such symptoms, but we weren't sure. Jonah's EMG (nerve conduction velocity test) left little doubt. He too would have to deal with the progressive weakening of his legs, braces, and the inability to run with his friends. I recall watching him playing soccer with his MSI soccer team. He would run with his upper body cranking along and his lower body struggling to keep up. He didn't fully understand yet; this was the way he always ran. I smiled to watch his efforts, but they broke my heart. As he progressed through elementary school and middle school, he came to understand that some activities would be beyond his reach. Cooperative physical education teachers kept him from using disability as an excuse for non-participation. He was not yet wearing braces, but their need was becoming more apparent.

Throughout Jonah's K-12 schooling it became more and more obvious to me that Jonah was blessed with two major advantages in his coming to grips with the limitations of neuromuscular disease. One was his incredible personality that charmed all with whom he had contact. Capable of finding humor in any situation, he rarely seemed down or depressed. Secondly was the relationship that he developed with his mother. She was a continuous role model for him as well as a source of information. It was clear to me that they would and could share feelings that were unique to them. I occasionally felt left out, particularly in high school and college days when I would accuse Marilyn of spoiling Jonah and of not being objective when dealing with a father-son disagreement. It took me a while to realize that my feelings of exclusion were really expressions of jealousy of a relationship I never had with my son and maybe a little anger of CMT for depriving me of some of my early dreams for father-son ball games, etc.

I still feel that my relationship with my son is a work in progress. I have great admiration for his energy and his independence. I love the adult he has become. Our communication has improved and continues to improve. I am in awe of the work that he does and know that he is now a role model for many of his friends and colleagues. I don't have a handicapped son. I have a son with a limitation who can do anything he sets his mind to. My heart is no longer broken; rather, it is full to overflowing.

Name: Melissa Lalonde
Years known Jonah: 5+ in this life, but our souls have definitely met in previous lifetimes
Title of connection to Jonah: My connection with Jonah is one of friend, sister, peep, emotional guide/healer.

I often forget about Jonah's disability; it is just part of who he is. Jonah does not hide it, he is open about it and we talk about it. I see it. He shares his struggles in getting braces to fit comfortably. It is at these times that I often stop to think about the daily obstacles he faces. He has to wear socks all the time (even when it is 100 degrees outside), has found a few pairs of shoes that do well with his braces and sticks with those, he rarely wears shorts and I have always assumed it was to cover his braces but am realizing I have never asked. Jonah, is that why you rarely wear shorts??

Jonah asks or accepts help as needed, like when we went shopping for a dress shirt for him to wear when he married two of our closest friends. I helped him button and unbutton various shirts he tried on and it was the totally natural thing to do. I have offered a hand when hiking unstable terrain with him. His disability is incorporated into who he is. Jonah's disability does not stop him from trying things/doing things/having experiences. If anything, having a disability only seems to push him further/harder. I guess that is my experience. My sister sums it up well: "he walks like a cowboy."

The Stuff of Dreams

"I figure, the faster I pedal, the faster I can retire."

—Lance Armstrong

Chapter 9

The Stuff of Dreams.

(The following is my journal from RAGBRAI. The Register annual great bike ride across Iowa. The register is Des Moines main newspaper.)

It is 8 a.m. on Thursday morning, and I am in Iowa. I am in the street and on my bike, waiting for my friends to put the finishing touches on their gear. I have a generally straight face on me; I throw out a joke here and there for good measure, but inside, with all sincerity, I am nervous and on edge. I am about to leave this house and set off on bike for three days, amidst thousands of people, and across greater distance than I have gone yet, by a long shot. I am concerned as a man with a disability, and I am concerned as a man who loves to lie on the couch. On both fronts, I am justified. Even with all of the months of training, anticipating, talking, and worrying, I am totally unaware of the grand adventure I am about to set out on. The next three days would test me, break me, and build me back up again. On every level.

We leave our friends' house, and bike about five miles to meet up with the beginnings of the official Ragbrai route, and it's estimated 11,000 riders. I have my bike, a Trek Antelope. An old and solid model. Bought on Craig's List for $80, and "Jonahfide" for about $200 more. I have a picture of my grandfather on the mainframe for inspiration, a sumo squeaky toy for kicks, and handlebar speakers that plug into my i-Pod for sanity.

I ride for about a half hour and all is calm. We are on side streets and it is quiet. Then Dave, my friend and bike guru, pulls up next to me and says, "Hey, I think we found Ragbrai." I look ahead and see an undeniable flood of bikers, all in flow. There are so many of them, and the flow never stops. You get the feeling right away that you could stand there for hours and bikers would just keep coming by. By the hundreds. We make our way to the river of peddling maniacs and set our vibe. I am nervous, and a bit glad to no longer be thinking about it all, but to be doing it. I set my right foot in the pedal cage, grip my handle bars, say one last prayer to God and whoever else might be listening, and off I go....

Rider on! It is one of the most important pieces of Ragbrai vocabulary that the riders come to learn. Whenever you are entering into the route, you yell out, "Rider On!" This lets the other riders know that you are about to enter the flow and that they should look out. Later, I would come to coin my own version of it:

"Rider wobbly coming on!" There is a booklet that all participants receive filled with the etiquette of the ride. The proper form of Ragbrai riding, the various pieces of Ragbrai language to be mastered, and the layout of the route. I read this booklet cover to cover, twice. It is interesting to note that while the information in that book seemed to be mere words in advance, they became vital pieces of success when actually in the ride. For example, the maps. They are just maps beforehand. But each day of the ride, you cling to them as proof on how much f**king further you have to pedal before you can f**king stop pedaling. (Side note: There is a lot of cussing at Ragbrai. When you are exhausted and going uphill in the Iowa heat, you just say F**K a lot. Total strangers look at each other at the top of a steep hill and say "F**k." So in these reflections, you'll have to deal with it. Now back to the f**king point.) The most important information in the book is the vocabulary you learn, in order to be always aware of what is coming up ahead, or from behind. *Rider On* = a rider is coming into the route. *Slowing* = a rider is preparing to leave the route by slowing down first. *Rider Off* = A rider is leaving the route. *Car Back* = A car is coming from behind to pass ahead. *Car Up* = A car is coming from ahead to pass behind. "*On your left*" = A rider is about to pass you on the left side. You can figure out *On your right* and *In the middle*. *Rumble* = You are about to cross over those rumble strips in the road that make you jiggle like a massage chair. The vocabulary is interesting, but what is cool is to see how it jumps off the page from words to life. The lingo, while monotonous at times, is truly there for safety. You come to appreciate those who use it, and you come to use it yourself so others will appreciate you. I quickly came to feel that all of the riders were working as a team to ensure a safe experience for everyone. People work together. And the more you feel that, the greater the feeling of responsibility to that. Everyone pretty much looks out for everyone else. When someone breaks down, all who pass them offer help. When someone falls down, people instantly stop and help them back up.

So this verbiage is the main language of the Ragbrai flow. You need to know when someone is about to come into the route. You need to know when someone is about to leave it. You want to know when a car is coming in either direction, both to avoid it, and to prepare for the inevitable condensing of the riders to make room for it. I always loved the car warnings because you could literally hear them flow down the road. You start by hearing the people way behind you yell out, "Car Back!", then you hear the people right behind you yell it, then you yell it, then those just ahead of you and so on and so on. It's like the wave at a ball game. A little more than is needed, and a very safe way to avoid any incident. Once on the route, you can relax a little bit; it is crowded, but not often cramped. The roads, for the most part, are car free. And the riders themselves are a sight to see. You have everything from pro riders to amateur riders who think they are pro, little kids on bikes, seniors, and every age in between, abled, specially abled, on single bikes, tandem bikes, three, four, and five person tandem bikes, decorated bikes, unicycles, low riders, incumbent bikes, extra tall bikes, bikes with sails, boxcar-covered bikes, thousands of them, in every shape and size. The riders go all out. A lot of veteran riders come with a team. They dress up the same or wear similar jerseys. The team names are always funny, seemingly including a bike reference mixed with a sex reference mixed with a drinking reference, and the outfits are even funnier. It's a circus on wheels. The route is lined with houses, townships, small towns, and large towns. Iowans really come out for the show. I must have passed a million lemonade stands, each kid cuter than the last. Others do it up and really put out a spread. You can always find snacks, drinks, and Iowans looking to cash in on the flood of consumers. There are some vendors who have become famous in Ragbrai over the years. Best known is "Pork Chop Man". This old guy who sets up his pork chop stand every day and yells out, "Pork Chops!" People rave about them, and he is beloved. For me, the idea of a pork chop during my ride made me wanna hurl. There are also a lot of tenderloin sandwiches. You see, Iowa is pig country. You get nasal evidence of that every so often. Many Iowans set up chairs in front of their houses and just wave as you go by. It's like watching a great live movie. I loved saying hi to every one of them. They are friendly people and the love makes the pain subside, if only for half a second.

 The main flow of each day is town to town. You pass about 5-6 towns per day with an average of 8-12 miles between them. Your first big town is usually breakfast, a few towns later is lunch, and a few later is camping for the night. Between the towns are houses, snack/drink stands, some Amish communities, and many many miles of rolling cornfields. If you need to pee, you either wait for the next town, luck out with an Amish port-a-potty, or go to God's gift, the cornfields! They are an accepted form of relief along the route. Right by the road, you just walk in about 3 stalks and try to forget about *Children of the Corn*. (Side note: you get a few feet into a corn field and you literally feel cut off. It's a little eerie in there, no pun intended.) I loved the scenery. It is beautiful in Iowa. Simple, natural and beautiful. Hot as fuck, and really wonderful. With you is your bike and whatever can safely and not too heavily attach to it. Ragbrai transports all of your camping gear and stuff to the next evening's camp grounds. The bitch is that you are only allowed one bag. It can be a big one, but you have to fit everything for the week in it or on it. So I packed my big backpack and tied my tent and sleeping bag to it. Overall, for the madness and size, Ragbrai is pretty well-organized, and the participants are great people to spend some days with. It is a world all its own. The organizers, participants, and Iowans all work together and all seem to love it dearly. It is a win-win for all involved and one hell of a good time....

A quest for Independence. Day one. Ragbrai is a seven day ride across the state. Two of our crew were in it for the whole week. The other seven (myself included), were joining them for the last three days. So my day one was Ragbrai Day five, and so on. Once I got into the flow of things, I felt pretty good. I had music playing, I was feelin' good on the bike, I was well equipped and instantly got into having so many interesting and friendly people to say "hey" to. The day would log sixty-three miles and climb about 1400 feet in elevation. Our first town was Denver, Iowa. Funny, being from Denver, Colorado. It was super cool. Most towns really put on a show. There is decoration, music, food, and a ton of bikes and people. There are no locks; for the most part, all of your stuff is safe just left wherever you find space.

I had ridden about eighteen miles so far and was sweating heavily in prime Jonah fashion. I walked into the bar where my crew had planned to meet. There I bumped into Barb, my dear friend who is a Ragbrai veteran. It was so good to see her. A friendly face went a long way after a morning of unfamiliar and nervous tension. She would prove to be my Ragbrai angel, popping in on me when I needed it most with a hug, a word of encouragement, a mother's touch, a slice of pie, or a funny Ragbrai friend who knew of a secret shortcut and had a story to tell.

After resting and drinking a lot of water, we were on the bikes again and off we went. The day was tough. It was really hot and very sunny. It is hard to stay hydrated in that situation. The other tough part of that first half of the day was the introduction to the eighth wonder of the world: Iowa hills. You see, there is magic in them. They keep going up and very rarely come back down. Maybe the heat and exhaustion had a hand in it, but it felt like most of the day, I was climbing up small to medium hills and never coming back down. I must have ended the trip on Mars. The cell phone and "the plan" are your two best tools for finding your friends during each day. Every person has their own pace with riding, and besides some brief check-ins, you usually separate on the route. So when you are together, you are always talking about what "the plan" is for the next meeting in the next town. The hard part is that you don't know what the layout of the next town is, or any set point to meet. So you often end up with plans like, "we'll meet at the first tree on the left, or the first bar on the right." That's when the cell phone comes in. You enter each town and there are several thousand people just hanging out. You pray for cell service, which is very sporadic in Iowa, and you call or text and try to find each other. More times than not, the cell in combination with the plan worked out o.k.

After lunch in Dunkerton, we met later in the afternoon in Fairbank. I was beat. I had cycled about forty miles. I was wet from sweat. My hands were sore from leaning on my handlebars and my knees hurt. I found my friends and was very happy to see them. It is amazing how your priorities shift under physical need. When I first saw my friends, the words that came spilling out were *shade, sit, water*. More often than not, the needs of your friends are the same, so we found our shade, filled our water bottles, and sat the fuck down. It feels so good to sit on the ground after being on the bike for so long. Talking with friends and comparing the journey and discomforts was very refreshing and reassuring. As we sat there, up walked Barb with five slices of pie. We ate the shit out of them. It was so good.

It was in that resting moment that I came to learn another constant reality of Ragbrai: the longer you rest, the longer you want to rest. And the sooner you get your ass back on that bike, the sooner the day will be done and you can recoup at the campground. So you make deals with yourself at every rest. Constantly calling out how much longer you will sit there. It's a tough battle of you versus you. Typically, though, you rest appropriately and get going when you should. You always go fill up your water bottles before leaving any town. Most towns have free pipes to do just that. When I left Fairbank, I had two towns and twenty-three miles to go. It turned out to be one of the two toughest stretches for me of the whole trip. I was hot. Very hot. I was starting to get dehydrated. You become aware of this when you feel like you have to pee, but when you do only a little comes out. It's a drag. I was, by this point, running behind. I was usually behind my friends. I am generally a slow biker with spurts of excellence. I was stopping a lot just because I couldn't go forward anymore. My roadside breaks got more frequent, about every three miles. On one of them, I took the first of two total falls, both of which were falls, not crashes. Both occurred when I came to a stop and did not dismount correctly. The average bike seat is high enough off the ground that you can't just stop and put your foot down like when you were a kid. You have to stand on one pedal and lift off of the seat to get your feet to the ground. On all stops but two, I did that just fine. On this one, I stopped the bike, and simply fell over. Nothin' but a little skinned knee and a small blow to an already exhausted ego.

During this time I began my love affair with my bike bag. It is a medium sized bag on the back of my seat. I loved it because it had my comfort needs in it: power bars, energy shots, and a washcloth for that feeling of home. The bag is your only real luggage during the day. You resort to it constantly, like your whole life is in that one little bag. A few miles at a time, I made it to the final town. Once there, I found my friends and collapsed on the sidewalk. My friend Ben carried my bag for me. My tent was already set up and I just sat on the ground for a while, trying to ease my mood and recapture my sense of humor. After a while, I did just that. We were in Independence, Iowa, camping in the field behind a school. The school was a shower and recharge spot. Once the feeling came back into my legs and smile, I went to shower off. It felt so good. It was a poem of water. It was heaven's shower.

After my shower, as I was getting dressed, a man walked up to me and said he wanted to take my picture the next day. After a few moments of thinking this guy had come to kidnap me, he explained that his name was Jack. He was a teacher for the first grade, and he had a student in a wheelchair. He had seen me riding with my braces during the day and he thought it would be so cool to get a picture of that for his student to remind him that he can do anything he wants to. I gladly agreed to be photographed and went back to my crew at the tents. That night we went into town to seek food and chillin. We ended up at a crowded pizza place and ate ourselves happy. We had a few beers and talked about our day. It was good. I felt accomplished. I felt glad to be off the bike. I felt glad to have good friends with me. I felt good. I also felt the first of my sincere thoughts that my riding was over. The day had been a lot harder for me than I had expected. It was farther than I had ever gone and in much greater heat. It just wasn't that fun by the end of the day. It was work, and I didn't like it. The thought of two more days was an instant trip to Quit-Town. I just couldn't accept the thought of doing two more days of that. And the word on the street was that the last two days got really hilly and tough. I went to bed that night with a plan to get up, bike a few miles and then cash it in. That plan felt good to me and I slept like a drunk in a king-sized bed.

Group, as defined in *musical terms:* a section of an orchestra comprising the instruments of the same class. The group I traveled with was by all means comprised of a similar class, and on several levels: humor, support, ailments, and courage. There was me, Jonah B. Disabled and relatively new to the biking world. Still getting my groove on with longer distances. Then you have Derek, one of our Iowa hosts. An occupational therapist with a hell of a good heart. Derek ruptured his Achilles tendon a few months back while playing soccer. About three weeks after he announced his injury to the team, he sent out an e-mail with pictures of the moon boot he had designed and created. It was a huge stabilizing boot for his leg to which he drilled a metal plate onto the bottom of. This metal plate latched onto the clip pedal of his bike. Derek rode 163 miles over three days in that thing. Oh, and did I mention his wife Mary Pat, who is six months pregnant, and who rode about 90 miles over two days. And she complained the least of us all. Then we have Dave, the common tie to this motley crew, the founder of the feast. Dave had been struggling with tendonitis in his right knee for several months now. He was one of two in our group who attempted the entire week. He made it five days straight through pain and struggle and covered over 340 miles in that state. His wife Sarah, who is smaller than any of us, was the one soldier of our crew who accomplished all seven days. Coming in just under 500 miles. Words don't begin to cover it. Representing the truly healthy and normal members in our crew were Chad and Nellie, a married couple who spent all three days on a tandem bike. I paid close attention to them because I was sure that they were going to be all over the place and falling down. Not because they are lesser riders, but because the tandem bike is a whole different beast. It requires a constant flow of communication and uniformity. Turns are harder, quick adjustments are trickier and overall, it is a little less safe. Yet these two were as smooth as smooth could be, easily pulling ahead of the group when they needed to. They were champions. Lastly was Dave's brother Ben (Mr. Cowan to those who know him well), and his girlfriend Meghan. The two of them had the sweetest bikes of anyone in our crew. They also had the sweetest skills. They both finished first out of our circle each day, getting in several hours before the rest of us. They pushed through each day and basically never let up—an amazing feat for the weather and miles. They were our resident bad-asses.

This crew of ours was a great group for me to be with in regards to my personal journey with this ride. They were supportive beyond words. They were constantly throwing out encouragement when we would pass each other. They were always waiting on me in the next town, and when I would pull up, they would grab my bike from me and lead me to shade. Sarah pulled up a hill twice as fast several times just so she could jump off of her bike, grab her camera, and snag a picture of me flying by. Ben carried my luggage from the truck to the tent. My tent was set up for me at the end of the first two days when I arrived, thanks to Dave, Sarah, and Chad. They all pitched in and packed up my gear and tent on the last day so that I could get an earlier start and improve my chances for finishing. Nellie organized a singing crowd at the top of the toughest hills on the last day. They did all of this for me and asked nothing in return. They were simply happy to help. They were pulling for me. It was this group effort that really put me over the top. Ben came to me at the end of the second day and said, "That's it man, if you can make it through 2 days, you're finishing tomorrow." It was a bar I was proud to rise to meet. Our crew showed a smaller reflection of the Ragbrai way: looking out for one another. Taking care of each other. Laughing through the pain. Supporting the ups and downs of it all. I couldn't have been more blessed.

Believe *me, Ray, people will come. They'll come to Iowa for reasons they can't even fathom. They'll turn up your driveway not knowing for sure why they're doing it.*

They'll arrive at your door as innocent as children, longing for the past. Of course, we won't mind if you look around, you'll say. It's only $20 per person. They'll pass over the money without even thinking about it: for it is money they have and peace they lack. And they'll walk out to the bleachers; sit in short sleeves on a perfect afternoon. They'll find they have reserved seats somewhere along one of the baselines, where they sat when they were children and cheered their heroes. And they'll watch the game and it'll be as if they dipped themselves in magic waters. The memories will be so thick they'll have to brush them away from their faces. People will come Ray. The one constant through all the years, Ray, has been baseball. America has rolled by like an army of steamrollers. It has been erased like a blackboard, rebuilt and erased again. But baseball has marked the time. This field, this game: it's a part of our past, Ray. It reminds of us of all that once was good and it could be again. Oh ... people will come Ray. People will most definitely come ...

Day two. On paper, the day is set to log 64.7 miles and a climb of 2,400 feet. But in my mind, I had already worked out another plan. I was reeling from the pride of my first day and figured I had proven enough. I factored on starting the day, riding a small chunk of miles and then cashing it in. I was sure that my plan was going to go just like that. I didn't see it as giving up; I saw it as saving myself from two more days of pain and struggle. We rolled out of Independence and made our way east. The morning was a decent ride. I was sore from the day before, especially in my hands, wrists, and forearms. This is one of the two areas most affected by my disability, and my adopted riding style had me leaning pretty hard on the handlebars while I rode. Up to this point Derek, Mary Pat, and I were riding together. The others had pulled ahead. It was just the limping and the expecting pullin' up the rear that day.

We made it to the first town—the breakfast town. Winthrop, Iowa, one of my favorites on the route. It's a small little town that came out in force to meet us. They had a band playing, and a full made-to-order breakfast burrito table set up. It was like morning hungry heaven. Over breakfast we got to talking to a gentleman who was riding his fifth or so Ragbrai. There with his wife and five children, all of them riding. While I literally inhaled my burrito, he and I were chatting about the difference between east and west in regards to human decency. "I have a theory!" he said. "I think it is a matter of population. There are more people on the east coast, and as the population rises, that's more and more people you have to be nice to. If you were nice to all of them, you'd be saying good morning for hours on end. After a while, people just stop doin it." I don't know if I buy that theory, but I was happy to hear it. It was one of hundreds of interesting conversations I had over three days. How rare a treat to be able to be exposed to that many interesting and friendly people all at once.

Then who walks up but my angel Barb with her good friend Kathy. Kathy is a school superintendant and one of the most down-to-earth people I think I have ever met. They come and sit with us, and we eat and talk about our sluggish morning. Barb and Kathy are smiling, and upon asking them why, Laura proceeds to pull out a map of the day's route and shows us a shortcut that will shave about twenty miles off of the ride that day. I smiled like 7-11 had just offered to put a slurpee machine in my kitchen. Derek and I looked at each other as if to seek out the brave lad among us who would demand that we stay the original route and not cop out that way! Thank God there wasn't a man among us, and we swiftly accepted Barb & Co.'s offer to cut the corner. I figured this may be the ticket to keeping me in the game, at least for one more day.

After breakfast, we mounted up and proceeded to cut through a neighborhood to get to our shortcut highway. The Iowa police are not too keen on short cutters because they can't keep an eye on you and ensure your safety, but we made it to our path and off we went, accompanied by several hundred riders who either knew Laura or knew how to read a map. We were on a ten mile ride to the next town of Manchester, as opposed to the other 10,000 riders who were on a thirty mile trek to that same town. My enthusiasm soon passed, as I realized that this ten miles stretch was still hot and still very hilly. To be honest, my arms and hands were really starting to hurt. It was getting to the point that I had to switch hand positions every ten to fifteen seconds. Whenever God gave me the slightest downhill, I would ride one-handed and give one of my arms a brief rest. My mood was starting to drop and my thoughts of quitting began to rise again. About the only treat of that stretch of ride was Laura. She and Mary Pat and I were riding together. Talking to her was really great. She is one of those people who is so true to life that it is infectious. At one point on the ride, when some clouds had moved in and the temperature cooled a bit and we were on a nice flat stretch of road, Kathy looked at me and said, "This is a good day to be alive. This is a thinking day." I dare say I won't forget that moment.

The closer we got to Manchester, the worse I felt. I was grimacing from the pain. I was dying to get to that town and just sit. We pulled in and called the others in the crew who did not know we had shortcut. We found out the crew was several miles outside of Manchester, so we parked ourselves by the entrance and waited for them. This was going to be my one chance of the ride to welcome my friends as opposed to the opposite. We had lunch in this cool little town that resembled main street Mayberry. During lunch, I looked at Derek and said to him that I didn't think I could go on with my hands and arms. He got the occupational therapist look in his eye and disappeared into the local drugstore, emerging moments later with a bag full of gauze and tape. He said he wanted to try and tape me up and relieve some of the pressure. I figured it couldn't hurt. He spent the next 20 minutes going to work. A few passersby were watching. Derek knew his stuff. This was no joke tape job. When he was done, I looked like a superhero with forearm guards and gloves. My wrists did feel strong, so I decided to give it a run. I had nothing to lose. Although Derek had taped me out of my immediate quitting plan, I was sure I could just cash it in later if I needed to. But the tape worked like a charm. There was an instant difference in my level of pain, and therefore, an instant uprising in my good humor. Derek, Mary Pat, and I hit the road with a new found zest. We were cookin'. The next 3-4 hours were one of the best stretches of my ride. It was cloudy, which was a blessing. Cool and a little breezy. I had good friends with me, who liked to laugh, which was a blessing as well. And we were on our way to Dyersville, Iowa, which excited the hell out of me because it is the location where one of my favorite all time movies was filmed, *Field of Dreams*. Now that my arm pain was under control, I was also able to tap into the saved energy from our shortcut. In moments over the afternoon, I would just start to cook. It would come on at the bottom of a downhill and into an uphill; I would feel this calling to not just push up the hill, but to kick its steep ass. I would lean forward a bit, shift the force of my energy to my core center and legs and keep my upper body stiff and strong. In those moments, I felt like a king. These bursts of power would get me up about half way to three-fourths of the way towards the top of the hill. They were exhausting pushes, but exhilarating as well. In those moments, the sheer joy of riding kicked in. You are absolutely one with your bike, you have the wind in your face, and you are blowing past other riders. It's a taste of power—a very healthy type of power, your own. After a few stops and a great small town visit with our friends, we pushed through to Dyersville. Before I knew it, we were there. I was so damn happy. The shortcut had made the day tolerable for those of us with buns in the oven and plastic on the legs. It was perfect to have the short day in the middle.

The entry into Dyersville was my favorite of the ride. They had set up a tunnel going over the road that leads into town. It was called "The Tunnel of Dreams." And inside were stalks of corn and plastic blowup baseballs hanging everywhere. It was a great feeling to ride through it. The town's people were out in numbers clapping and welcoming us. It was a moment Mr. Costner would've been proud of. We made our way to the others who had found a shady spot to set up our chairs. We arrived to an applauding crew of our friends. It was a great way to finish that day. Without Derek, I would not have made it. Thanks, brother. Dave had spent his first day off the bike. His knee had spoken the final word. Although we all knew how disappointed he was, he spent his day setting up our tents for us and getting beers so we could chill that night. It was over the top.

Even in his disappointment, he still looked out for his people. The word on the street was that a church in town was putting on a spaghetti dinner for interested riders. A few of us went over and stood in a very long line to get a square meal for $8. The meal was good, I was craving pasta, and the dessert was Amish pie. During dinner, a local Dyersville resident came to pour us some water. We got to talking with this nice guy and he informed us that the church was probably going to have fed 4,500 people before the evening was done. Pretty amazing. We asked him about Field of Dreams. He told us all about it. First of all, he owns the farm right next to the field in the movie. He said that in the last scene of the film when the long line of cars with headlights is pouring into Ray's farm, if you look in the upper right corner of the screen, you should be able to see his house. He also told us that the field from the movie is actually owned by two different farms, split somewhere down the right field line. The farmer who owned the infield kept it just as it was in the movie, half corn/half baseball diamond. The other owner plowed it off and planted new corn over the whole thing. After a few years, the first farmer was making a killing on tourists wanting to see the site, that the second farmer plowed his corn and remade the rest of the baseball field. So now, when you come into Dyersville to see the field of dreams, there are two roads that take you there, and two farmers who will accept your money to see the spot.

We went to see the cathedral after dinner, which was one of the more beautiful ones I have ever seen, and cool for such a small town. Back at the campground, it was an all out party. Evidently, the last full night of Ragbrai is a bigger deal than the finish of the race. This sucked for me because I had planned to hit the hay early and get a good night's sleep. Instead, I laid awake in my tent to the sound of drunken bike riders and a shitty cover band that actually did a Britney Spears song. Oy vey! I went to bed feeling for the first time that I may actually give this thing a run, but I was really worried about the rumors I had heard. Everyone was talking about how hilly the last day was—and steep hills to boot. For the first time on the trip, I was willing to admit that I might actually go all the way; the problem was that I didn't yet believe that I could.

Riding with a physical disability is obviously always a main consideration in my Ragbrai experience. Yet for some reason, it wasn't as much a thought on my mind in preparation for Ragbrai. I was concerned about my body holding up, but that was because of the many, many miles that I was slated to ride. I was also more concerned about being so close to so many other riders. Not because of my disability, but because of my freshman/sophomoric biking skills. It was once I actually got on the ride, that the disability began to come into my mind and into play. This is because I received a unique welcome from many of the Ragbrai riders as a result of my condition. You see, I am used to being surrounded by my friends, people who know my condition well, and who accept it purely. So much so that I forget about it at times when I am with them. To their credit, I feel pretty normal amongst them. But you put me in a pair of shorts, braces shining in the sun, amidst 10,000 strangers—10,000 biking strangers—and the picture begins to change. I was overwhelmed, to say the least, by the reaction I got over the three days. I would estimate about one hundred times that another biker commented to me in some way about their support of my riding with a disability. The reactions ranged across the spectrum. Many riders would simply pass me by and say things like, "Right on, man," or "Keep it up." Many of these never even turned to look at me when they said it. They just wanted to throw out some encouragement, and every time, it was greatly appreciated. There were a few interested and bold people who would pull up next to me and ask why I was wearing braces. I love those people. I always have. Those who ask what is on their mind. I sent about ten riders back into the world with a new found understanding of Charcot Marie Tooth disease. Then there were the boisterous encouragers. Like the old New Yorker I chatted with at a rest stop, every time he passed me after that he would scream out, "Look at YOU! You look GREAT!" Then there was this wonderful woman who biked by and told me I was going to be her inspiration for the next two days. And of course there was Jack, my friendly shower stalker who couldn't get enough of my endeavor. After a while, I must admit I felt a bit guilty. I wished everyone on that trip could receive such encouragement. It felt so good. Everyone on that ride deserved such praise. I suppose I see it as God's way to even out the score a bit. I have to wear braces and deal with additional discomfort, but I get a ticket to connect with people. I get the opportunity, although unintentional, to inspire others. That is a sweet gift. And Ragbrai really brought it to light. If some of my effort came from inspiring others, then great. I wasn't gonna let em down. And there were others who inspired me. There was talk of two different blind riders. They would be riding tandem with sighted partners. Talk about guts. I also had the great pleasure to witness a brother/sister team in action. They looked to be about 55 years old. He was in a wheelchair and did not have the use of his legs. She appeared to be fully abled. They had geared a bike to the back of the wheelchair. He sat in front and had a hand pedal to crank away on, and she was behind riding her ass off. It was a sight to see.

 A special note in this journal has to be made here in regards to my friend Dave. I thought about him the entire time I was on the bike. Why? Because it is thanks to Dave that I have become a biker again after about twenty-five years away. It was Dave that fell in love with biking. It was Dave who shared that love with me. It was Dave that eased me into the idea of biking. It was Dave that researched and found my first used bike. It was Dave over the past few months who has slowed himself down and started from scratch with me as I have overcome my discomfort and found my groove. He has been a constant support and strength to my riding and to my confidence as a rider. If it were not for Dave, I wouldn't have been at Ragbrai, simple as that. It is thanks to him that I walked away having had one of the greatest physical experiences in my life. Thanks, Chachi. Needless to say, I was in this ride for the challenge to my physical abilities. I suppose I just wasn't aware of the rewards that were waiting for me. My friends, and also the many strangers of Ragbrai, made me feel amazing over the course of the ride. The encouragement I received was extremely helpful to me and my success. For a change, I felt special in the best of ways.

A few weeks before Ragbrai, Dave had told me that on or about the third day of riding, the body starts to catch up with itself. You start to feel into what you are doing. I remember thinking that was a load of horseshit, but as the alarm went off at 5:30 a.m. on day three, the first thing I remember feeling was pretty good. I wasn't shocked by the alarm; I wasn't in misery by being awake at that hour. I remember thinking, o.k., time to go. 57 miles and a climb of 3200 feet was a waitin', so up I got, I got dressed, and as I looked up at the still dark sky, I felt as though I had already given the day over to the powers that be. I was in their hands. And because of that, I was free not to worry about control, of continuing or quitting. I simply felt at peace that my job for the day was to ride and for a change, not to think. The plan was for Mary Pat and I to take off early and ride together. The rest of the group would pack up our stuff and theirs and follow behind. Derek was up and ready with the tape and the superhero transformation began. When he was done, we loaded up our water bottles, said peace out to the peeps and off we went in the noticeably cool and quiet Iowa morning. The plan to leave early paid off right away. There was a palpable difference at this time in the morning. The riders were quiet, focused and swift-moving. The air was cool, the mood was smooth. Mary Pat and I both realized that we were glad to have the jump on the day and on the thousands of other riders. On our ride out of town, we were talking with a guy from Texas, a really friendly and slightly heavy set gent who told us that he was gonna finish this day for his Dad. Why, we asked? "Because when I told him I was doing this, he told me I was crazy and that I had bitten off more than I could chew. So I'm going to finish no matter what." He was my kind of guy.

The other beautiful gift that awaited our early morning trek was a series of about five to seven long downhill stretches. It was like heaven. There was alot of smiling going downhill, a great way to start the day. You stock up on good mood when you go downhill. God probably knew what the afternoon had in store and was trying to build us up first. Mary Pat and I both felt so good that we blew through the first town and pressed on to the second. I would ask her from time to time how the baby was enjoying the ride. It would appear that for the most part, the baby dug the motion of the bike and slept while she was riding, waiting for the kicking party at the end of the day. After about twenty miles of riding, we arrived in Cascade, Iowa. Just outside of town there was a senior center. The residents were all outside giving out free water and cookies. Mary Pat and I decided to check it out. It was very sweet. I took a picture with their roadside spokesman. As you entered the town, there was a big sign that said, "Ask us how Cascade saved the Ringling Brothers circus!" So I did, and found out that in 19 and 75, the Ringling Brothers Circus broke down about an hour outside of Cascade. They were going to be late for their next show and so the people of Cascade got together and trekked out to help them along, loading all of the people and animals and such into their trucks. To this day, if you show a valid Cascade ID at the Ringling Brother circus, you get in free. We ate in Cascade and called the crew to meet up in the next town, which we did, in Bernard, Iowa. Once we got there we circled the wagons and began to map out the rest of the day. There were two towns left, and both were about thirteen to fourteen miles of biking away. I was already tired and starting to dread the afternoon.

This is a good time to take a quick break and tell you about two funny Ragbrai things. One is butt butter. This is nothing you want on a bagel. This is a cream that bikers know to help with the rash that starts to develop on your ass after a few days of riding, implying that the dry friction of your two butt cheeks constantly rubbing together causes the rash, and butt butter, as our team has come to call it, helps to soothe the friction. I, being a new rider, just couldn't bring myself to butter up, and now that I have been through it, let's just say that my nickname next year will be country crock! The second and more prevalent Ragbrai factor is the rumor mill. It is a mighty mill, and it is crankin' all of the time. There are two main subjects of rumors that you hear about throughout Ragbrai. 1. Lance Armstrong 2. The terrain that lies ahead of you. The Lance one is funny. He was at Ragbrai this year, and has been for the past few. He drums up more water cooler chat than O.J. "Did you see Lance?" "I totally saw Lance," "Lance is surrounded by a posse of mean perfect bikers, he's so untouchable," "I did shots with Lance in Cascade" "My cousins' nephews' second grade teacher saw Lance two days ago." It is quite a stir. He is the king of bikeville for sure. The other rumor really hammered home on this last day. There had been rumors all week about the last day, and particularly, the last half of the last day. Everyone seemed to agree that it was the steepest stretch. Everyone also agreed that there was a strong downhill at the very end of the ride. The details though, were a lot less defined. I can't begin to explain how many versions of the final stretch that I heard. Everyone and their mama had a different story to tell. Derek and I were playing off this and trying to stretch it as far as it would go. "I hear there's cash at the end." "I hear they helicopter you to the finish line." "I hear Tom Petty rides beside you and sings 'Free Fallin' as you float in." Derek pushed hard and made it to the end by the time the rest of us were half-way and prepping for the final push, so there were some phone reports from him. An insider, a trusted source. But you come to learn that every rider is subjective. One man's "small hill" is Jonah's f'n Everest.

    We set out for the second to last town. It was definitely hilly and I was definitely getting tired. And just before the next town, I had a small mental meltdown on the side of the road. I think I had just about had it ... again. Plus I was hungry, and very thirsty. I had about three miles to go to the next town, but in that condition, it felt a lot farther. The last few miles into town, I was literally fanaticizing about curly fries and cheese sauce. I saw it so clearly in my head that I could taste it. We finally made it to LaMotte, Iowa. The crew was waiting at the entrance and screaming for us. They were great. They took my bike and we went to get our grub on. It was a great town for lunch with a nice shady, grassy town center and a bar-b-que buffet set up. Not only was I about to eat, but finally, it looked like I had found the place to throw down on some Iowa corn. I bought a hot dog, two ears of gold and a Gatorade, and we went to sit down. People used to make fun of my Grandfather because every time he ate something, he would say, "that is the best damned _____ I have ever had." I gotta tell ya, in all of God's sincerity, sitting there in LaMotte, I had the best damned corn I have ever tasted in my life. It was such a moment; I had to look over to Sarah for back-up. "Is it me, Sarah, or is this the best damned corn you have ever tasted?" Sarah confirmed it, and we went on with our messy selves. About twenty minutes later, it was decided that the time had come to press on. I wasn't happy to hear it, but I was anxious to get the monkey off of my back. We loaded up and started on our way. Mary Pat had decided it was time to call it a day, so she and Derek drove to the end to meet us. It was down to me, Sarah, Chad, and Nellie. We decided to finish this thing together.

    The final stretch was about fourteen miles, mostly straight uphill. The first thing out of town was a steep hill and it just got worse from there. After a few really tough climbs, we hit what I have come to call, "The Mother Load". It was technically one hill, but it was broken up into three parts. You would climb this forever hill, and when you got to the top there would be a very small flat stretch and then another very steep, very long hill. Three in a row. You kind of go into a zone during these stretches. You are aware of the effort you are putting in, but other things fade. No one really talks. There is a lot of heavy breathing. I tried not to look ahead because it was like the top of the hill laughing at me. I just kept pedaling, and pedaling, and pedaling. And when I had had enough, I pedaled some more. It was pure and crystal monotony. I was going very slowly, so it was literally one pedal at a time. I had to swerve a lot to keep from tipping over. There was no speed or momentum to keep me straight. It was madness. I could've read the Torah in the time it took me to get up there. I remember getting to the top of the mother load and the peeps were cheering me on, and I rode right past them and onto the grass, I hopped off the bike and passed out face-down on the grass. I think I lay that way for five minutes, just trying to sense if my legs were still there. I remember looking over the face of another total stranger who was also laying face down. We laughed in our pain. It was a bonding experience. I remember thinking that I did it. I had made it up that thing. I was bitching from the top. It was a good feeling. I started to sense the taste of the end. If I could make it up that thing, I wasn't gonna stop. I was starting to really feel tough.

After a small break, we pushed ahead. Hill after hill, and several more mini mother loads. I remember Barb telling me about a game she had played to keep her mind occupied going up a hill. She thought Mary Pat's name was such a clear sign of Catholicism and that she knew many other Mary-somethings. Barb decided to run through the alphabet and come up with a Mary name for each letter. I thought this was a swell idea and so I chose to give it a shot on my way up a crazy long hill. It actually worked pretty well. The last thing you want to do when fighting to get up a hill is think about it, so the distraction proved to be a good one. Not all of my names were proper names, but I didn't care. I was making it up the hill. I wasn't about to fight with myself over grammar. And now I know that if I ever convert to Catholicism, my wife and I will be blessed with Mary Oprah, Mary Xylophone, and Mary Uganda. The other good thing about that stretch was that Jack, my teacher friend, caught up to me, pushed ahead to the next hilltop, and caught about five shots of me going by. I was really glad for that. There are two moments I remember from those hills, one was when this dreadlocked hippie kid came sailin' past me, he had a trailer with full-sized speakers on it in the middle of a very steep and long incline. His system was playing Will Smith's, "Getting' Jiggy With It." It sounded so damn good. Will and that kid got me up that hill.

The other and potentially best Ragbrai moment for me was with the brother-sister team on the wheelchair-bike. We had been passing each other leading into the hills. When I was going up each hill, I would usually pass them. They were working so hard to get up each one. It was amazing. I would always throw out some love when I went by them, and he would throw some back, but his sister was too busy to talk. She was working—standing on her pedals and throwing her whole body into each push. It was tough to watch. On this one particularly tough hill, I saw them up ahead, and as I was watching them, two bikers came flying past me from behind. They were cookin' up the hill, clearly trained riders. I watched them slow when they saw the brother and sister. I watched them each pick a side, pull up next to the sibling team, and reach one of their hands out to grab hold of whatever they could grip on the sibling bike. For the rest of the hill, the four of them rode as one. These two guys had one hand on their own bike and one on the siblings' bike. I was sobbing. It was quite literally one of the most beautiful things I have ever seen.

The rumors of the final push being downhill were close to true. It wasn't all downhill, mind you, but it was relief compared to the stretch we had just been through. Those last few miles gave me some much-needed reflecting time, and a few moments alone with the corn to work it all out and soak it all in. There was one major downhill right near the end. I flew down that sucker, screaming and laughing out loud. Sarah said I flew past her and she was doing 30 mph. It was a great rush at the end of three tough days. Just about the time when my ass was cussing at me and my hands were about to liquefy, we turned a corner and saw "Welcome to Belleview" sign. Up ahead were Derek and Mary Pat, standing on the side of the road with cameras. We were done. We had made it—each in their own distances, each with their own version of challenge. I was really peaceful in that moment—something about accomplishing that which you are sure is outside of your reach. We loaded up the bikes, took off our bike shorts and went down to the Mississippi River to finish the thing off ceremoniously. Those who ride the entire week start in the west and dip their back tire in the Missouri River and at the end, they dip their front tire in the Mississippi. I chose to dip my sweet head in that there river. After three days, about 163 miles, and many ups and downs, I was done. And so, the journey ends ...

Iowa makes you smile. And cuss, and quit, and see, and understand, and break new ground. There is something that happens when we are broken down. When our squeaky-clean defenses are stripped away. When the task at hand and the labor involved are so grand, so far beyond our comfort that we simply go into a zone. This is what happened to me in Iowa. It was so much more than a bike ride, so far beyond a physical challenge. It was a test. A test whose questions could not be studied for. A test whose grade would simply report if I kept going or not. I quit in my mind about fifty times during Ragbrai, promising myself that I could stop after the next town. I realize in retrospect that I wasn't able to conceive finishing such a task. I could only conceive smaller chunks of it. So I only promised myself to finish those chunks. I gave myself the comfort of quitting after them. And that is how I made it through Ragbrai. That is how I passed this test—one chunk at a time. Although I couldn't see it all in the moment, I see clearly now that I received many gifts out there on the road. I got three days totally away from my car. I got to understand what Dave always says about cars being cages. I got to talk to total strangers because there was nothing dividing us. I got to be so thirsty that water tasted like love. I got to be so hungry that I ate out of need, not desire. Food tastes so damn good when your body actually *needs* it. I got to spend three days amidst the rolling green of Iowa, amidst cornfields whose tops reflect the exact contour of the earth below. I got to feel the power in these legs of mine whose notoriety often comes from their weakness. I got to fall and get up again. I got to feel at total peace. I got to feel what it is like to release control and just be, to let life dictate. And beyond all of these gifts I received, I believe one to be the greatest: I was taught a lesson on this trip that even when you are so sure that you can't accomplish something, there is a chance that you can. If you had asked me on day one or two if I was going to finish, I would have said no, and I would have meant it. I believed with every fiber of my being that I wasn't up to the challenge. I was sure of it. And yet, I did finish. Despite my sincere belief in my limitations, I surpassed them. The message it sent me was one of faith. It was, in essence, the very definition of faith, the belief in that which you cannot see. It was a remembrance that even if you believe something can't and won't happen, that it still can. That we are not the final word in all matters. We go so far, and life carries us the rest of the way. I ended my Ragbrai experience with that feeling inside of me, and that feeling caused me to be calm and serene. My eyes were relaxed and true, and to put it simply, I was happy. There is great reward waiting out there beyond our comfort zone. One undoubtedly has to make it through the unfamiliar and the uncomfortable to get there. But for those with the gumption and courage to venture out, at least from time to time, there is great reward.

(From left to right: Sarah, Chad, Nellie, and me.)

The Ultimate Tour Guide

"Now I'm starting to think that it's not about what happens to us, it's how we deal with what happens to us...."

—Anonymous

Chapter 10

The Ultimate Tour Guide

Jonah and his mother, Marilyn

The most important person to me in relation to my disability, besides myself, is my Mom, Marilyn. She is a beautiful person inside and out, top to bottom, a fellow participator in the journey of life with CMT, and to put it mildly, the greatest mentor of how to live with a disability that anyone could ever ask for.

It is hard for me to sense where my own strength with this disability begins and her influence upon that strength ends. The best way that I can describe it is that if you peel away a layer off the top of my strength and courage, there you would find my mom, at the root of all my ability, at the core of my perspective, and at the very foundation of my entire outlook on my life with a disability. The most impressive part is that most of her teachings were not of the verbal kind. Most of her lessons were not preached. They were shown to me through action. They were gifted to me because of my closeness to her. I had a front row seat for the hardest working band in show business. My mom has the same disability as I do. She has struggled with it the same way I have. Throughout my life, she always wore braces, she had pain, she was constantly challenged, and yet, she was the busiest mother of anyone I knew. You would simply never have known by looking at her that she struggled with a disability. She was always on the go and seldom slow about her life. She worked, parented, and socialized with the energy of two healthy moms. She was simply a champion, a hero in the most down to earth sense of the word. And by being her son, by watching her, I was given the gift of her outlook. Her wisdom came down to me in the form of three lessons.

1. <u>**The disability isn't in charge, we are.**</u>
    The message was sent to me in many ways. In her energy level, her activity level, her tolerance level—all of which are off the charts. She made it clear through her actions and lifestyle that she was the determining factor in the pace of her life. The disability would have a say, but not the final say. The tool with which my Mom was going to beat it back was attitude. She simply never let it get too big in her head or get in the way of her pride. And therefore, she was always in charge. She cried in moments. She cursed the pain in moments. She had to go to get her braces fixed a thousand times, but those things never stopped her, they were mere road bumps. I am proud to say that I have carried on this tradition. I have maintained the pace she set for me. And when my braces or pride or ego or pain start to get to me, I think of her. I think of the example she set and continues to set, and I push on. Through pain and frustration, I keep moving. I am the result of the momentum created by her.

2. <u>**Be open with others. Be a teacher.**</u>
    My mom was open about most things. She was the person that everyone felt comfortable talking to. People opened up, confided in her. She has always had that energy about her. It was no different in regards to CMT. She walked with an air of comfort with it. She didn't shy away from it. She wore it. It was her. It was who she was. The many times I witnessed someone ask her about it, I bore witness to her instant openness. She would talk to others about it. In minutes she would have someone educated and understanding her. It was amazing to me. I paid attention to how comfortable she made others by choosing to talk about it. If you shy away, it makes it bigger somehow. It is hard to say that one lesson she taught me was any more valuable than another, but I will say that this lesson was a big one. It has molded the very style with which I carry this burden. I am thankful to have been shown this light so early, as it has helped me to show others the very same light. It is contagious in the best of ways. The idea that whatever you have that is unique to you carries a responsibility to show others, to teach those who don't know and to help other people to understand one of the many differences out there. She helped me to see that we were gifted the chance to teach!

3. **There is a gift hiding in this disability, for those who choose to see it.**
Those who know my Mom and especially those who know her disability would agree that there is a glow about her. There is a glow in the way she has chosen to deal with her challenge. This glow is the gift. She has taught me through her life and her ways that there are palpable gifts to be received from the acceptance of a challenge. You get the gift of insight. You get the gift of sensitivity towards others. You get the gift of seeing how interdependent we truly are. You get to be the teacher and the taught. You get to inspire others with your courage. You get to be different. These are gifts. And while not always seen as so, in moments, when I experience my mom dealing with this disability, I can see she is glowing from these gifts. And if you see this glow, you are experiencing the gifts as well.

One of my Dad's favorite poems is called "You Have To Be Carefully Taught." It is all about how children are taught to be the way that they grow up to be. Children aren't born with a predisposition towards hatred and bias and fear. They have to be repeatedly taught these things. I always believed in that poem, and I also think that it applies to my life. I have received many compliments over the years as to how I handle my disability. I am complimented about my physicality, my attitude, my energy, and my thoughts. And while I love to hear those precious words, I have always felt that it was simply the result of how I was taught. I was brought up this way. It wasn't this miraculous choice to be who I am; I followed the plan laid out for me. I'll give myself no more credit than that I saw a good thing and had the courage to follow it. I entered a brand-new world of physical challenge and simply had the ultimate tour guide. I was trained and taught and shown the ways of true courage. I was blessed with a wonderful mom.

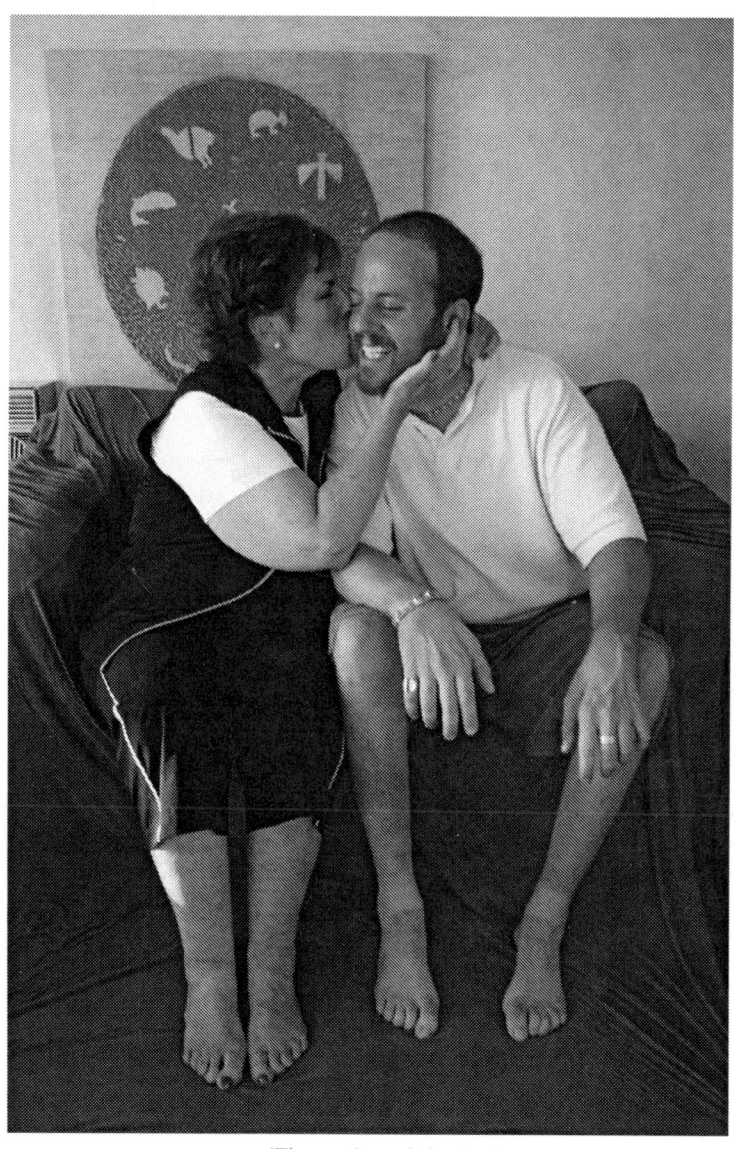

(The apple and the tree)

The Forced Reliance on the Rhythm Within.

Ω

The color of life, in all its shades. Seen clear at times, and others, it fades.
Aiming to match scripted accolades. When it shouldn't be aiming at all....
Taking each step in total perfection. Lending my feet to cautious direction.
Yet intent disguises in total deception. The truth of the fear to fall....
So go ahead and trip, you'll only hear the sound. Of the thud of your body when it hits the ground.
At least it's real and far more profound. Than the hollow echo of fear....
Yes, truth comes shining through, you see. Like the most reliable cavalry.
Peace is not as far as you thought it might be. More often, it's oh so near....

—Jonah Berger

Chapter 11

The Forced Reliance On the Rhythm Within.

Caged, barred, trapped, sentenced? Enlightened, allowed, shown, entrusted? Without the ability to always rely on the typical senses, one must accept a forced reliance on the rhythm within. With my ever-decreasing "strength" comes an ever-increasing call to hear the internal music, the strength that comes from knowing truth, from feeling righteousness. And less from clearing the hurtle and finishing first.

I am forced to walk through life with a body of courage and strength, set upon feet of clay that can crumble at any time. My arms, strong and able, are finished off by hands struggling to pick up a penny. There is strength in the middle, weakness on the ends. If only my chest could button a shirt, or my thighs could hold up my feet. Like a piece of gold only an inch out of reach, like a chance to love missed by a second's tardy arrival. It is easy to find frustration, but harder, it would seem, to find peace.

I walk with feet of dead weight. I walk by raising my leg and flopping my feet down. I walk with the internal strife of a mind that moves three times as fast as the feet. I walk with a youthful knowledge of freedom and expression of ability, locked further away in time in a body that can no longer accomplish the remembered deeds. I am aware of how to be smooth with women and know that all the knowing in the world won't take the braces off of my legs, that all of the knowledge of cool won't stop me from tripping in front of her. All of the understanding of strength won't fill in my thinning hands and shattered façade.

Or maybe it is that I was sent for a reason, that physical challenge is my enlightenment to deliver. Maybe I was sent to help slow others down. To ease the rush of normalcy. Maybe I am a hand-crafted mirror to reflect appreciation of health and strength back onto others. Maybe I am special in a righteous sense, and less so, a sad one.

To truly evolve, to truly accept, to truly be true, one must rely on the rhythm within. One must see the strength that comes in the true acceptance of weakness. One must allow that strength can be found even where a lack of strength resides, that deficiency can be an opportunity for growth. That maybe it is the responsibility of those who are different, to teach of their difference to others. Maybe it is important to remember that each and every person in this world, by the sheer definition of our individuality, has special needs—needs that are special to them.

Do we share some in common? Yes of course: to be heard, to be held, to be loved, to be needed, and to be understood. Yet there are more specific needs that become special to each of us.

Mine, among others, is to be listened to when I vent my frustration about my challenge. Mine is to be understood when I throw my leg brace against the wall at the end of a long day. Mine is to be understood when I cuss at the failed attempt to pick up a coin off the ground from lack of finger strength. Mine is to ask a total stranger to button up my shirt, as I stand before them bare-chested and late for a formal affair. Mine is to curse zip lock bags, mine is to fight screw tops I can't budge, mine is to spend ten minutes trying to get a pill out of the child-proof (and seemingly disabled-proof) packaging. Mine was to struggle back in the day while holding chalk and trying to write on the board (where was dry erase when I needed it most?) Mine is fighting to get my license out of the tight pocket of the wallet. Mine is to be challenged at times, to be comforted at times, to be respected for my own attempts to challenge my own limits, to expect those around me not to resort to pity with regards to me, and rather, to take advantage of the opportunity to learn from me. Mine is to always seek ways to find greater acceptance and larger amounts of comfort with my own condition. Mine is to be allowed to wish to the sky at times that I didn't have this disability. Mine is to be granted the moments of denial and anger. Mine is to be allowed to walk this path in the best way that I can. These are my special needs.

These are mine. A blind man has different needs and, a deaf woman, still others. A child with Down's syndrome has a very special set of unique needs, as does a thirty year-old female with autism. A rock star that lives life on the road has special needs, a single mother of four as well; a homeless man has special needs, and make no mistake about it: so does a rich man. Oprah, my Uncle Gene, my friend Horace, the CEO of Pepsi, a small child, the lottery winner, the school teacher, a prisoner, the African, the southerner, the lazy, the hard worker, the one in the spotlight, the one in the dark, the one who makes the fries, the one who seems to have it all together, the one who seems to be falling apart, the poet, the young, the old, the mentally challenged, and the physically disabled ... they each and all have special needs, needs known only to themselves. We are all exactly alike in regards to our possession of uniquely special needs.

I have special needs. As I grow older with this disability, I come to rely less on wanting what I can't have. I come to spend less of my precious energy fighting that which I cannot change. I save more of my precious energy for the real fight, for the walking on the path of the disabled, for the extra strength it takes to just barely keep up. I have come to see that it takes a great deal of ability to be disabled in this world. It takes physical and emotional courage. It takes a heightened endurance for discomfort. It takes an ability to tune out the constant reminder of walking in braces. It takes a sharp courage to attack physical feats that would unnerve an abled body. It takes the belief that anything can be accomplished once you let go of the notion that there is only one way to accomplish things.

The core explanation of my way is that I have come to hear the truthful sound that plays within me. I have come to see that beauty is truly not about eyes or skin or pounds or decorations. Beauty is about knowing truth. Beauty is about being at peace with the truth. The rhythm within is the song that plays for me when I am caught up in the haze of trying to be something that I am not. It's the beat that reminds me to follow, in stride, the path of truth. I am a disabled man; I have the opportunity to accomplish almost anything I set my mind to believing in. I need help. I am 6' 2". I cannot always make it alone, and often times, I prefer not to. I have climbed the 2nd tallest peak in the lower 48 states. My eyes are brown. I am strong because I deal with my weakness. I am strong because I moved out to Colorado from Maryland on a notion. I am strong because I don't allow my weakness to define me. I am strong because I have acted in plays to a full audience. I am strong because I can talk about my weakness. I am strong because I can lean on others. As I continue to walk this path, I will, like everyone, have my triumphs and my defeats. To recognize that and never stop pushing forward is the song that my rhythm within is playing.

I have no choice but to rely on my internal rhythm. I cannot rely on running to feel speed. I cannot rely on strong hands for quick buttoning. I cannot rely on smooth moves to attract the opposite sex. I cannot will my feet to pick themselves up when I walk. I cannot keep up with my friends all of the time. I cannot feel good about this all of the time. I cannot will this away; I must meet it head on and accept it. I have to accept it. Not only that, I have to *smile* at it. I have to always strive to listen well, set my course, and go grooving and stumbling on my way down the road.

The journey continues....

978-0-595-47168-3
0-595-47168-4

Lightning Source UK Ltd.
Milton Keynes UK
UKOW051104141111

182034UK00002B/193/A

9 780595 471683